Don't Judge My

Until You Know My Been Through

Author- Rev. Charles Earl Conaway Sr.

Co-Author Dr. Glennell Conaway Ed.D RN

authorHOUSE®

AuthorHouse™
1663 Liberty Drive
Bloomington, IN 47403
www.authorhouse.com
Phone: 833-262-8899

Published by AuthorHouse   01/27/2021

ISBN: 978-1-6655-1490-3 (sc)
ISBN: 978-1-6655-1491-0 (hc)
ISBN: 978-1-6655-1508-5 (e)

Library of Congress Control Number: 2021901731

Print information available on the last page.

Any people depicted in stock imagery provided by Getty Images are models, and such images are being used for illustrative purposes only. Certain stock imagery © Getty Images.

This book is printed on acid-free paper.

Because of the dynamic nature of the Internet, any web addresses or links contained in this book may have changed since publication and may no longer be valid. The views expressed in this work are solely those of the author and do not necessarily reflect the views of the publisher, and the publisher hereby disclaims any responsibility for them.

CONTENTS

FOREWORD

The celestial and divine occupation of preaching and teaching radiates a surplus of feelings; some of them are feelings of joy, sorrow, and passion. We experience joy because God has decided to look at us through His lenses of love and see our purpose and potential, and he gracefully places us into the ministry. It is a joyous feeling that we experience, but the ministry can also bring inevitable sorrow. Why sorrow? To be honest and forthright, our intentions to be of service can be met with resistance, rejection, and even ridicule! But despite the consequences, we are yet driven by duty to cultivate the areas we serve. Yes, there are joyous moments, and there are times that we will walk through the valley of sorrow and distress, but the question is, what is it that drives our service when our sentiments are fluctuating like the weather of Chicago? How do we continue to teach and preach when our euphoric moments create an atmosphere of ease, but then we are swiftly and suddenly thrown to the hard floor of catastrophe and disappointment? How do we continue to serve while celebrating the victory of our Christian companions, but then we must privately deal with our vicissitudes that perpetually presses, depresses, and even oppresses us? The answer to this series of inquisitions is this, our PASSION. Our Passion for the task is what is going to keep us fueled in the good and frustrating times.

What Is Passion? According to the urban dictionary, the word passion is when "you put more energy into something than is required to do it. It is more than just **enthusiasm** or excitement; passion is the **ambition** that is materialized into action to put as much heart, mind, body, and soul into something **as is** possible." Passion is also defined as a "strong or barely controllable emotion."

If I had to sanctify these definitions for Passion I would say that passion "is a voracious spirit that energizes our commitment to live, love, and labor for kingdom advancement."

Our Job is to teach and preach regardless of whatever state we may find ourselves in because we possess a thirst that cannot be quenched and a fire that cannot be extinguished. The Holy Spirit that resides within us is who creates and stimulates our Passion.

What is teaching and preaching?

In my definition, teaching is the didactic process by which people are divested of their former practices and developed by biblical principles according to His plan. Preaching is an oral communication of divine certainty with a viewpoint to persuasion.

These two tasks require a sanctified passion; without it, the assignment would be unproductive. In John chapter 21 in Jesus' post-resurrection moment, Jesus was having breakfast with a few of his disciples, and the text says in verses 15-17, "So when they had dined, Jesus saith to Simon Peter, Simon, *son* of Jonas, lovest thou me more than these? He saith unto him, Yea, Lord; thou knowest that I love thee. He saith unto him, Feed my lambs. He saith to him again the second time, Simon, *son* of Jonas, lovest thou me? He saith unto him, Yea, Lord; thou knowest that I love thee. He saith unto him, Feed my lambs. He saith unto him the third time, Simon, *son* of Jonas, lovest thou me? Peter was grieved because he said unto him the third time, Lovest thou me? And he said unto him, Lord, thou knowest all things; thou knowest that I love thee. Jesus saith unto him, Feed my sheep."[1]

I believe these verses highlight a few things about the Passion needed to teach and preach God's word.

1. Our Passion is what makes Ministry a Priority.

Jesus asked Peter **_"loves thou me more than these?"_**

What are the "these" that Jesus is referring to? Many have offered us their opinions on this text and I agree with the nuances of interpretation. But in my own exposition and hermeneutic, I believe that Jesus wanted to readjust Peter's focus. Remember that Peter had resorted back to his former occupation that Jesus had called him from to be "fishers of men." But in Peter's response to the crucifixion, he resorted back to what he loved and what he was good at. Jesus asked him, do you love me more than these fish, this boat, and this equipment? Jesus shows us through Peter's catechism that ministry must be a priority. Even in times of hardship and disappointment, we all must be invested into kingdom work and that we cannot resort back into

---

[1] _The Holy Bible: King James Version_. (2009). (Electronic Edition of the 1900 Authorized Version., Jn 21:15–17). Bellingham, WA: Logos Research Systems, Inc.

our zones of comfort and leisure when life and labor gets difficult.

2. Our Passion calls us to Minister to all People.

We must take notice of 2 things in the commentary of Jesus, he says in verse 15, Jesus says, "Feed my lambs," and then in verse 16, Jesus shifts and says, "Feed my sheep."

Lambs are a new, young and feeble form of the species that are not yet matured. Sheep are the older form of the species that still are growing. Jesus is saying to Peter and to us who desire to minister through teaching and preaching, that we must be able to minister to both genres. Those who are new and young in the faith and still like a lamb have weakness in their legs and are unstable at times and we must minister to those who may have the tenure but yet have some kinks and imperfections that still need to be worked out. This service type is tedious, but it requires an unquenchable spirit if we shall effectively minister to all people.

3. Our Passion in Ministry calls us to Serve beyond Preference.

John exposes the use of two different Greek words for love. One word is "Phileo," and the other is "Agapao." These two verbs sound the same but are different in expression. Phileo is a term that emphasizes fondness and a liking, and Agapao reveals a benevolent and unconditional love. Jesus asked Peter this question about love to shift Peter's love from being that of a fondness (phileo) to a love of benevolence (agapao). Love is what undergirds us in our ministries even when we may not be fond of the circumstances surrounding us. After all, this is the love that God has for us, and it is through this love that he faithfully ministers unto us.

If we maintain our Passion, a voracious and an unappeasable volition in our call to teach and preach, God will be glorified, the church will be edified, and the devil will be horrified.

By: Reverend Jarvis J. Hanson, D.Min, and D.D.

ACKNOWLEDGEMENTS

My thanks and gratitude goes out to my Pastor Rev. Dr. Jarvis J. Hanson, D.M. My help meet, personal nurse, BFF, worse critic, and my best cheerleader and love of my life. I'm speaking of none other than Dr. C (Glennell Conaway), *Ed.D, M.Ed., MSHSA, BSN, RN*. Both Pastor and Dr. C shared the same thoughts about this writing. That thought was that I needed to proceed with having this published. My intentions were for this just to be a manuscript to be given out to a select few who were going through melodramatic (intense) times in their life. Now, I realize that God's intentions were greater than mine. Pastor Hanson wrote these exact words to me "Ministry has to be looked at globally not just locally. This especially holds true in your case you being an Associate Minister. You have a greater platform that can be used not only in your church but across the city and the country. Don't minimize the testimony that God has given you just to the local church level when He has given you something that can bless people globally". Last but certainly not least I also would like to thank my primary care Doctor of over fifteen years in her encouragement in this writing Dr. Mandakini. Pokharna MD.

INTRODUCTION

"WARNING! WARNING! WARNING!"

To those who might be reading this writing for entertainment this is not the writing for you. I was inspired by the Holy Spirit to do this writing in one of my "Private Room Moments". Which you will find out what this is if you continue to read. As a matter of fact, I'm not even clear on how to label this writing. Is it a book, a memoir (biography), auto biography, or book of testimony? I really don't know. Not even why I'm (we are) writing it. I don't even have a clue as to who it may even benefit; Dr. C and I are not looking for financial gain, fame or any of that stuff. But there is one thing we (Dr. C & I) do believe is that it is written under the guidance of the Holy Spirit due to the fact that I haven't any writing experience at all. But my brothers and sisters over the years that Dr. C and I have walked this Christian journey together if nothing else we've learned to be obedient. So let it be known as you continue be it known this writing is under the guidance of the Holy Spirit. Just like the author of the bible this is not written in any chronological (consecutive, order of events) I wrote it as it was given to me by Him. When I review this writing there is something I noticed (and I just did). Yet, as my Pastor (Rev. Dr. Jarvis J. Hanson) would state in some of his sermons. "It's shallow enough for a baby to swim and deep enough for an elephant to drown". Meaning just about anyone can read this and get an understanding as to what the authors are conveying (passing on) to you. This is raw no professional editing or none that stuff. So let the faith journey (voyage) begins!!!!

DEFINITIONS

COPD- Chronic obstructive pulmonary disease (COPD) is a chronic inflammatory lung disease that causes obstructed airflow from the lungs. Symptoms include breathing difficulty, cough, mucus (sputum) production and wheezing. It's typically caused by long-term exposure to irritating gases or particulate matter, most often from cigarette smoke.

HERNIA- A hernia occurs when an organ or fatty tissue squeezes through a weak spot in a surrounding muscle or connective tissue called fascia. The most common types of hernia are inguinal (inner groin), incisional (resulting from an incision), femoral (outer groin), umbilical (belly button), and hiatal (upper stomach).

CORONARY HEART BYBASS- Coronary bypass surgery redirects blood around a section of a blocked or partially blocked artery in your heart. The procedure involves taking a healthy blood vessel from your leg, arm or chest and connecting it below and above the blocked arteries in your heart. With a new pathway, blood flow to the heart muscle improves.

PETECHIA- Petechiae are tiny red, flat spots that appear on your skin. They're caused by bleeding. They sometimes appear in clusters and may look like a rash. If you have tiny red, purple, or brown spots on your skin, they could be petechiae. They're not a disease, but a symptom. A number of things can cause them to happen, from a severe coughing fit to an infection.

OXYGEN

Oxygen is delivered to your cells and tissues through your lungs in order to keep your organs healthy. Normal blood oxygen levels are between 93% to 99%. If you have a respiratory condition such as COPD or the flu your oxygen saturation level can decline and supplemental oxygen can be used to treat the condition. Oxygen is normally prescribed when it falls to 90% and below.*https://www.webmd.com*

MY STORY

Rev. C.E Conaway, born on February 19, 1951 on a rainy afternoon at 3:50pm in Cook County Hospital Chicago Illinois. Born into the union of Herman and Mahalia Conaway. He is the baby of five siblings. Herman (deceased), Velma (deceased), Margaret and Harold. At the age of nine months I was removed from my biological parent's home to be raised and reared by my Aunt and Uncle Sylvester and Ethel Mae Riley. I won't bore you with a lot of the growing up process. Things were relatively normal. Although I will point out the fact that God allowed me to experience the elements of growing up (girl's, partying, gangbanging, drugs, drinking etc.). When I look back and think things over even then I realize that I was under his divine protection even at this early stage in my life. Saying that to say that he allowed me to experience these things growing up but only to allow me to be able to put them into my religious resume, but not allowing none of them too consume me except smoking cigarettes which I will address later. It was the only thing that stuck with me. This was to be used as a part of my calling in the future (you see God plans way ahead of us). He would only allow me to go so far and it would get to the point that I no longer enjoyed it. Now mature I realize that I only did these things to belong. In this life we all have to identify with something or someone whether it is mischievous or good just to fit in. Rev. J.E Hopkins a great commentator of the gospel would often state if you don't believe in something you will fall for anything. I vividly remember taking on my new birth (John 3:3) at the age of nine on the 3rd Sunday afternoon in August at Calvary Temple Baptist church located at 4426 S. Princeton in Chicago Illinois. I remember the Preacher (the late Rev.C.Harris) standing in the pool located in the basement of the church, clothed in his black robe saying in obedient to the great head of heaven "upon the profession of your Faith my dear brother I baptize you in the name of the Father, the Son & of the Holy Ghost". What was really strange about my baptismal was that no family members were there, no not one. Looking back on life and at my household structure, to my recollection the only two people in my family that attended church were my grandmothers on both my Aunts and Uncles side. I never even remember attending a funeral at a church always at a funeral parlor (what a spooky place to go to in those days even by the smell of flowers you knew that you were in a funeral parlor) I would spend days afterwards having bad dreams. Thanks be to God for allowing me to get over that fear considering all the home going services I have to attend in this day. Grandma Riley knew there was a divine calling on my life at my early age. She had a nick name for me and she was the only one ever to call me that and no one else ever did until I accepted my calling. The nick name was very simple and to the point it was just simply 'Preacher'. When my Uncle Riley would talk to her or go visit and I wasn't present she would send word to tell her Preacher boy to be good. Auntie Mae told me one summer while visiting Grandma Rose in Leland Ms. That a Preacher came by to visit the family, there I was playing and minding my own business, this preacher decided that he would interrupt my play time by picking me up and said what a cute little boy. Well didn't I teach him not to interrupt a little boy at play I was told that I spat right in his face. After hearing this later on in life it was to my surprise that I didn't receive the whipping of my life. Instead Auntie Mae stated it was said by Grandma

Rose that boy is going to be a Preacher some day (talking about prophesying this was over 50 years ago). Uncle Riley and Auntie Mae didn't attend church; I believe it was at the age of eight they made sure I made it to Sunday School every Sunday. Bath on Saturday night Sunday School at 9am on Sunday morning some Sunday mornings I tried to play sleep sometimes even pretend to be sick, didn't work their comment was you will be alright. I actually begin to enjoy Sunday school thanks to a wonderful teacher by the name of Ms. Vaughn she required us to read and study our Sunday School lessons; she also rewarded us for our efforts (bibles and other gifts). I enjoyed BTU as well (hot chocolate and cookies). But being a child I still had to be mischievous, there were occasions when a friend of mine by the name of Rubin Bivens would decide we were just not going to attend on some Sunday's. As a result of our decision we would take our Sunday School offering and go to a restaurant to buy potato chips in a brown greasy bag. In addition, play coin machine games and return home at the time we were expected back from Sunday School. Lord and behold talking about it takes a village to raise a child was that ever so true then, and it needs to be implemented (put into practice) in our society today. On several occasions when returning, supposedly from Sunday School I was asked how it was and what did I learn. Well you already know the answer I had none. Some noisy (LOL) busy body had saw us, knowing we had no business being where we were because of the time of day and the way we were dressed. They knew our parents and squalid (tattle tail) on us. Well you don't have to guess the results of that (go get my belt). We could definitely use that type of village today. As a result of the village raising me and the whippings (corporate punishment lol) received I know I've turned out to be a better person in society not to say I was the perfect child or even young adult I did my do as stated earlier. But I never have spent time in jail (not even for a curfew violation) or experienced any of the other things that come with being contrary (different) from the way I was raised. I now thank God for the village and the corrective disciplinary action that was taken to keep me own a straight and narrow path.

Let me bring clarity to a previous statement I made, I said family didn't attend church I didn't say they didn't believe, because I don't know, I do know I saw Uncle Riley reading his bible on many occasions. Also let it be known that I called Auntie and Uncle Riley Mom & Dad. A little bit regarding my religious life. By the age of twenty five I had lost both sets of parents, what a devastating time in my life (only one knows how it feels only if they have been there). Children honor and cherish your parents while you can and parents do likewise. In book of Ephesians 6:1 it demands us to do that. Well it is often said that God will be whatever you need him to be (that is so true). Three years before this I had met this young lady through a summer work program named Glennell Hall. She was and still is a fine looking gal. You know what? She wouldn't even give me the time of day to make things short she didn't like my demeanor (the way I carried, conducted myself) but remember as I stated earlier this was only a camouflage in order for me to fit in. I just wanted to belong it wasn't the real me. Time went by not seeing or even communicating after about three years we once again made contact my feelings for her were still the same and guest what I was beginning to win her over, one day she invited me over to meet her parents (smile women do that to) in those days you didn't just walk into someone home without the parents at least knowing your name be it male or female well they seemed to take a liking to me. Even Grandma Nisie Green, now when you could win Grandma over in those days you had it going on, they would be the first to say that "Nigger" ain't about no good or ain't about nothing (just keeping it real that's what they would say). When ever I came for a visit I think we would make Glennell jealous because it seemed as if more time was spent talking to (Baby) Nisie Green than her (that's what I called her, now tell me I didn't have it going on). She would even call me into her room so she and I could talk she often referred to me as her "Nigger" and you had better not mess with me as a matter of fact. I was one of the few that could borrow money from her. She would say this is the churches money and I need it back because you know I ain't got any money. Although she was saved, sanctified and filled with the precious Holy Ghost she was a cutter if you made her angry. I think I know somebody who has that same DNA I'll give you the privilege of guessing who it might be. When I asked her parents to give Glennell and I their blessings to wed in April of 1972.

It was the late Rev.J. E Hopkins that often stated true marriages were arranged in heaven (can't you see God in this). What a day to remember! Due to the fact we were both raised to be self efficient and sufficient that's just the way we both are today. We were taught that we are to be the masters of our own destination. We asked her parents to do very little to prepare for the occasion. Just enjoy the moment. We decided not to have a big wedding in order to prepare for the day after. Food, clothing a roof over our head you know the essentials of life. As a matter of fact it wasn't until 25yrs.(Silver Anniversary) later that Dr. Conaway marched down the aisle for me to receive her. The wedding was presided over by the late Rev. Dr. John E. Hopkins. So to the youth of today slow down it's a long journey so take your time, aim for big goals in life, a fail is nothing but a try you might not reach the stars but at least you will be amongst them. Believe it or not if effort is put forward, where you are is better then where you were and what's to come is better than what's been. To this union four beautiful children were born Felicia, Arletta, Tanyanika & Minister Charles II and we now have 14 grandchildren and eight great grandchildren. Have to mention my daughter in-love Tiffany Conaway and son in-love Pastor Keith B Hayes we love them both dearly. Glennell joined New Nazareth in 1972 and was baptized by the late Rev. Ernest Sharper. Shortly after I joined let's be for real I only joined to see what my new beautiful bride was doing spending so much time at the church only to find out nothing but giving God the praise just as she does now but only harder and more. You see Saints when God blesses you your praise and worship should be greater, this should even be reflected in your prayers. I was always in and out of church. The late Rev. Hopkins hurt her feelings on one occasion he asked her where is that husband of yours, she replied at home. He stated he needs to be in church her response to Reverend Hopkins was that I was a good father and husband. He does those things he is required to do. Now you know Rev. Hopkins sugar coated nothing his statement was, saved people go to heaven not good people, Dives was a good man too according to the bible but he went to hell; boy was she hurt (There is no hurt like a church hurt and yes the truth hurts sometimes as well) but he was so correct. So after being in the choir, usher board, take note anything I felt wasn't right or met my standards I was out of church again. Finally I became a Deacon after Rev. Hopkins appointing. Then Prayer Band Director, what was that didn't have a clue as to what to do especially felt intimidated by the Prayer Warriors we had at that time. As God told Moses, open your mouth and I will tell you what to say (Exodus 4:1) for 13 years. The Prayer Band was never a large ministry in numbers but we were big spiritually. But Pastor Hanson has often stated "ministry is not predicated on your capability but on your availability" none of us are qualified but we must be authorized by God to carry out his kingdom building work here on earth. Thorough this ministry I have seen God at work. I have gotten many reports of deliverance, lives changed for the better, healing not so much as physical healing but spiritual, people have even stated to me that through this ministry their personal prayer life had been enhanced. Don't tell me what prayer can't and won't do. If you've got the faith God has the power. I thank the Lord for using me as a vessel in this ministry. He is due all honor, glory and praises I take no credit other than being just a vessel. I was a Deacon board member for a number of years (15?) I can't remember. I also served as Rev. Hopkins personal Deacon working with Sis. Lyra Crawford for quite a while. I learned so much from just being around this man of God that is now benefiting in being an ambassador (representative) for God. I vividly remember the last time I joined the church Mother Carmichael (one of the prayer warriors) told me that was the last time I would be out of church she had prayed that I stayed put. The power of prayer, I haven't left since. I developed all of a sudden a strong desire to become a Deacon loved praying, singing hymns and Dr. Watts. I wasn't sure as to how to go about expressing my desire so I confided in a Pastor named Rev. Emmit Jarman. He advised me that I was to be still that God would reveal to Rev. Hopkins if it was to be. Strangely enough some time after I'll never forget it was a Sunday in fact it was a Christmas Sunday. We were returning to church for broadcast quietly walking down the corridor Rev. Hopkins sticks his head out of his office says he needs to speak to me and my wife about something that next week. I believe it was on a Tuesday of that following week Pastor Hopkins sat my wife and me down this is what he stated. I have been watching you and have watched your spiritual growth. Being led by the Holy Spirit I'm going to offer you a position as a Deacon in the building of God's kingdom if you are willing to accept it, of course I accepted. His next question was to my wife asking her was she willing to support me in this part of my elevation in my walk with Christ, of course her answer was yes. Well I was voted in to serve as Deacon on the New Nazareth Deacon Board. My mentor and preceptor was Deacon Jack Waller his words to me when we went out on the communion field was son, always be prepared and most of all be real in your service to the people out here your job is to bring church to them. Going to work in the field became a passion with me. Myself, Sister Conaway (back then wives accompanied their spouses if they were a Deaconess), Deacon Hudson, Deacon Lucious Patrick, Deacon Lem Woods and at times Grandma Cora Taylor. We would bring church to the people, we were always prepared before entering a member's home as to who would sing a hymn, read scripture, serve communion and most of all pray. Grandma Taylor would get so filled at times that she would break out singing her rendition of "Holding my Saviors Hand". Sometimes we would leave the church at 11: 00am and would not return until broadcast time 4:00pm. Oftentimes, we would even have to grab a bite to eat in the field. We have served communion as far south as Matteson IL to as far north as St. Francis Hospital in Evanston IL.

I learned so much sitting at the feet of Rev. Hopkins words can't describe, and with Pastor Hanson it is just a continuation of my learning. I never will forget as long as I live the last time I served Rev. Hopkins communion on his sick bed. Because of our spiritual relationship no matter who was on the team to serve him and prayed he would give me this certain look and I knew I had to pray in spite of who just prayed. We had to have our private conversation with no one else in the room. The one thing I will never forget is he stated to me. He said to me that I have showed you and trained as to what to do and you know what you have to do (his exact words). At that time I didn't have a clue as to what he meant. I received my confirmation while attending a church service at a mega church (after his demise). They had altar prayer where you would go to a minister and tell them what your prayer request was. My prayer request was for our church family to remain together and remain on one accord. This minister not knowing me from Adam told me you have been told and you already know what to do (who knew it would lead to me becoming a minister I was quite satisfied with being a Deacon).

SPIRITUAL ORIENTATION

While going through what I refer to as spiritual orientation. The Holy Spirit within brought to my awareness that some things were yet missing. Based on the foundation that my ministry was to be built on (Prayer and Testimony) something's stilled had to come to past in my life. For the life of me I couldn't figure what it could possibly be. But at the end of the day (figuratively speaking) when things were quiet here comes that little voice from within; reminding of the things that had already transpired in my life in order to prepare me for the ministry that I had to carry out in His name as his Ambassador. He had been my financial advisor, marriage counselor (41yrs at the beginning of this writing), provided me with food, has always provided adequate living quarters for me and my family, and even given us many of the desires of our heart. After toiling with this from within myself I still found myself asking what He meant by this. Here comes that little voice again Y'all. It tells me you are a man of fifty-one years of age. You have not had a notable illness in your entire life. I had spent time in the emergency on very few occasions and the majority of those were on the account of family, friends, and never even stayed overnight for observation. So that is what's missing a testimony as to me being your healer, there for this has to come to past. Well its miracle time! It was sometime in 2001 I inherited a hernia in the left groin area of my body.

I was trying to be conceited or thinking this thing would go away. I ignored it quite a while only to realize that it wasn't getting better or going away. Nevertheless, as time went on it started to get larger, to the point that there was a bulge in my pants. Well finally in 2002 of January Mr. Conceited or even Mr. Arrogant went to the doctor and was told that the hernia was incarcerated (it had entwined with another part of the body) and surgery had to be performed. The urologist doctor stated based on what showed up on the ultrasound examination he could not see how I could even tolerate the pain that I should have been experiencing. Due to a previous medical conference that Dr. C had to attend in Nashville TN it was concluded that we could hold off a week on the surgery. Therefore, we headed out for Nashville a seven hour drive with me doing all the driving. Our arrival was smooth had a good dinner and a good nights rest. The next morning started out fine. The conference for the day ended early that afternoon as a result Dr. Conaway and one of her colleagues wanted to have lunch. I declined because I was beginning to experience an upset stomach, but to bring me something light to eat back. I realized that the seven hour drive to Nashville sitting in one position had upset things. Well after returning to our room sitting on the bed I felt a pain more excruciating than I had ever felt in my life (be it known that my pain tolerance level is very high). It was so bad it brought me to my knees even to the point of regurgitating. Well what was a short time that Dr. Conaway was gone seemed like an eternity.

Upon Dr. C's return to the hotel she found me almost in a state of shock (eyes not focused, skin was clammy and turning gray). When the ambulance arrived she was asked what hospital she wanted me to be transported to. Not being familiar with the hospitals in Nashville she suggested that they chose one with a good reputation for possible surgery (knowing I would need to have it). Well the one they chose was Centennial Medical Center. This was a beautiful hospital (the lobby had so much greenery one would think they were in an enchanted forest) and they seemed to have up to date computer medical technology (computer charting opposed (opposite) to paper charting. Observe the fact that this was in 2001 many hospitals today (2016) are just now converting into computer charting and medical records. Pretty much aware of what's going on after receiving something for pain (Wow what a relief that was) I heard Dr. C and the attending emergency room doctor agreeing that the surgeon needed to evaluate me. After the surgeon arrived, Dr. Chambers which we found out later he was one of the top surgeons in the Nashville area (look at my God at work giving his child the best). Dr. Chambers said yes I needed to have surgery but we might want to wait because the insurance company might not want to pay; because the hospital was out of their network. Well this didn't sit well at all with Dr. C I tell you the girl should have been a MD (medical doctor). She observed signs on my body (petechia) that indicated that there could be internal bleeding or a blood clot and to proceed with surgery we will worry about money when we get to that bridge. Dr. Chambers complied (in agreement with) her request stating the surgery would only take about an hour. Well that hour turned into 2 ½ hours Dr. C stated to me later she wasn't too concerned about the time as long as she didn't hear an announcement of "code blue" (cardiac arrest) in the operating room. Well after 2 ½ hours of surgery Dr. Chambers stated to her that he himself was so grateful (remember he is one of the top surgeons in Nashville his reputation is at stake) for her medical observation. He found internal bleeding and a blood clot that if I had traveled back home on a 6 to7 hour drive it could have caused hemorrhage or the clot to travel to my lungs or heart. That would not have been a good thing (but God protects his children) death could have easily occurred and for what? Over what, that thing called money.

THE BLESSINGS CONTINUE

Dr. Chambers said that my stay in the hospital would be three to four days. Oh' well because of my quick recovery (I see nobody but God in this). The insurance company said I had to be discharged the next day. Dr. C had checked out of the hotel and planning to stay at the hospital with me. I know none of you have been here but at this point our credit cards were maxed out and the credit card companies refused us extended credit (my God my God what are we to do?) you do know he will be a shelter for the homeless. We asked the nurse if there's a hotel or motel that the hospital recommends for loved ones that stayed with family in the hospital (this is a medical center not a regular hospital) at a reasonable rate and she gave us the information. Let me reiterate (repeat) that we are here on a medical conference. These people don't know us from Adam & Eve. Dr. C call's them to let them know she would not be attending the remainder of the conference and explained the situation; Look out God is going to show up and show out again.

Now Dr. C didn't tell them about the hotel situation but out of the blue the person on the other end asked where we were going to stay for the four days for my recovery this was Dr. Chambers suggested that I not ride home in a car for at least four days.

Dr. C. gave them the information and how much it would cost us (it was a reasonable price). The person on the other end told us to hang up and they would call us back. Well they did just that with another Hotel "Embassy Suites" they told us to check in just give our name arrangements had already been made. Talking about beautiful accommodation's it was actually a suite (out of sight) and newly built. To show you how small things can be so helpful. Dr. C called down to the desk and asked if there was a pharmacy in the area they replied yes that there was. Then they told her she need not drive there they would bring their car to the front lobby, take her and bring her back (what do you do, just stand and let God). Least I've keep you too long on this miracle and blessing let me close it out. After four days its check out knowing the company probably got us a break on the room (suite) rate we were all prepared to pay something not knowing how much and holding our breath. Fasten your seatbelt after a four day stay, meals prepared by a chef daily and parking, our check out balance was a whopping $25 for parking only somebody Shout hallelujah!, Thank you God for blessing us.

GOD TAKES CARE OF HIS OWN

In May 2003 I was admitted into Trinity hospital for respiratory distress which we thought was a result of having COPD. Well that was not the correct diagnosis. I was placed on a medical/telemetry floor being able to maneuver around without assistance but was on a heart monitor as a precaution. Well one morning two doctors were rounding for the shift to ask how I was feeling my reply to them was "Good." At that time they stated that they had some shocking news. The news was that sometime during the night I had incurred(suffered) a heart attack that the heart monitor didn't detect but the latest EKG revealed this to them. Look at God taking care of his own. Isn't one supposed to experience some type of symptoms etc. chest pain, pressure in the chest or shortness of breath? Well to my astonishment (surprise) I had none of these symptoms. After evaluation my doctor suggested that I be transferred to Mercy Medical Center. This was for two reasons, to perform an angiogram (an x-ray of blood vessels in the heart). Reason being if I needed surgery it could not be done at Trinity Hospital. Well as a result of this test Dr. Ranginain a cardiologist shared with me that I had two severely blocked arteries one 70% percent and one 85%percent and would have a heart double bypass surgery in order to correct the matter. Let's look at my God put his divine plan into action. I was scheduled to have surgery on April 2nd (I'm still in the hospital) at 12noon. However the day before the time was changed. Perhaps God wanted Dr. Matoya not to be fatigued when performing surgery on His child (LOL). Dr. C and I had our what if talk? This is the first time that I read the entire 30th chapter of Psalms which contains my favorite scripture Psalms 30:5. How befitting it was for this particular time in my life. David was telling God that he could not serve or praise him from the pit (grave). I made a commitment to Dr. C that when I came out of surgery that I would let her know that I was ok in my spirit due to the fact that I would not be able to speak. That morning while on my way down to surgery I suddenly had the fear of the unknown.

Therefore, I made my fear known to the Master (as if He didn't already know). Earlier I mentioned my earthly angel to you (Dr. C). I never mentioned my Heavenly angel to you. The babies at my church sing a song entitled "I've got an Angel watching over me". And they are there to protect me this is ever so true. Well her name is Aquafina, which represents water and water represents life. Although, I have never seen her she has made her presence known to me. She has allowed me to receive two white feathers from her angelic wings. For some unforeseen reason I was never able to keep them they just left out of my care. So after praying and talking to Aquafina this strange warm and calm feeling came over me. It went from the top of my head to the soles of my feet. The fear of the unknown was gone. I've only felt this one other time in my life. That was when my eldest brother made his transition and the family had to view his remains before public viewing would be allowed. The high risk factors involved had been explained to me because of my COPD. Well after 4 1/2 hrs. of surgery I was in post op (recovery). My first action was to keep my promise to Dr. C. I motion for pen and paper Dr. C had to translate to them as to what I wanted. Who asks for pen and paper after surgery? I guess they never heard or seen such a thing. Well after attempting several times to say I was ok in my spirit I failed. However, I was able to write "I

LOVE YOU" which nobody else could make out what I had written but her. The nurses and doctors were astounded they had never seen anything like that before (we serve an amazing God). Dr. Matoya had a concern about my respiration, feeling that he would have to leave me on the ventilator for at least 5 to 8 more hours. Well my brothers and sisters when man says no God will sometimes say yes. I'm told that I was only on the ventilator it for 3 hrs. Let us bear in mind that doctors are the resource but we must keep our focus on the Source which is the God Almighty you see they are because God IS. What's amazing about this is that I had the number one cardiac medical group in the country (Castle Connolly Top Doctors). Headed by Dr. Paul Jones here at Mercy Hospital in Chicago. Dr. Matoya and Dr. Ranginai are two of the group's top cardiology surgeons. Not to bore you with details but to inform as to how skilled they are. Most people that have heart surgery have a 6" scar which comes with an undesirable raised scar in surgery area which is a permanent scar. The same thing occurred in the area in which they remove the vein for the bypass graft procedure. Well I got the scar but guess what? It's almost invisible in both areas as a matter of fact the one on my leg is only about 1inch. I'm often asked by doctors who performed my surgery (God did it) but I give them the earthly surgeons name. They used bonded glue a new technique to close the wound the surgery area no stitches. Well after 5 days I was able to go home with no complications. How many can attest to the fact when God does something he does it well and complete.

MY PROVIDER

After being diagnosed with severe COPD, having a double bypass heart surgery I don't look anything like what I've been through. There is a proverb (saying). Don't judge my break through until you know my been through (praise God for the victory) it was decided that because of my medical condition it was advisable for me to retire. Let it be known I had already taken early retirement from Marshall Fields due to other issues not medically related. Look at God this all occurred before a 30 day period in which my health insurance would be terminated. Therefore my entire Medical bill was paid in full without even a copay ($200,000 +). Received unemployment (don't understand that because I chose to leave my employment it wasn't like I was unwillingly dismissed) but isn't that God taking care of his own. It was suggested that I also apply for disability. I had heard the horror stories that this was a long drawn out process. Dr. C initiated the call to the Social Security board. She explained to them that I had just had heart surgery and couldn't come in for an interview right away. God sends who you need and when you need them. The case worker on the phone stated that they would be willing to conduct the interview over the phone (keep in mind that this is the US government) and they would even call me. They followed through that next week as promised. It was about a 2hr interview (really it was). Questions about my doctors, medications, jobs, even the exact amount of my last pay check. I had to visit their doctor to evaluate me. I just knew I had lost my case then. Well guess what I was denied benefits. I immediately call to contest (challenge) their decision. I was told by my case worker (who I believe was saved and knew the Lord) to relax and be patient. To my surprise she stated to me that the benefits I was denied of were SSI benefits and that's not what she wanted me to receive because wouldn't give me much income (bear in mind I didn't know this person nor had I ever meet them in person). Well I finally received a letter stating that my unemployment was going to run out in a few weeks (watch God in action). Well it did run out just as they said. I was broke as a joke. I went to the cash station one day expecting to withdraw little if anything at all. However my God let me know the fact that he was my Jehovah Jira my provider. My disability benefits had kicked in with 5 months retroactive payments. With a lot of people this process takes years to complete if at all. I know people that this has happened to. As one great commentator (analyst) of the gospel (Rev. Dr. J E Hopkins) would frequently state. "It's best to have him and not need him then to need him and not have him" because God will take care of you!!!!!

KICKING THE HABIT

This is a short but powerful testimony. As I had mentioned earlier there was only one adverse (disapprove) I say adverse now, but at the time of use I enjoyed it. This habit I participated in for a time slot of about a 25 to 30 year period. Was this intended by God way back then for it to be part of my testimony (witness) for him today? Whatever, the circumstance we go. After being diagnosed (assessed) with COPD in the year of 2000 I was strongly advised to terminate this habit out of my life. Not doing so would get me to my demise (death) sooner. This was in their eyesight but God does things according to His own will. Being a little conceited (disobedient). I continued to smoke. Why did I continue this knowing I was told of the results it would have on my life? Because it didn't at that time seem to have an effect on my body or physical activities so I continued. My first sign of respiratory distress (not being able to inhale nor (exhale) the extra carbon dioxide from the lungs which makes it difficult to breath referred to as acute severe exacerbation(meaning to make something, worse in this case breathing). This occurred in the later year of 2000. Did I quit then? No still Mr. Arrogant or hardheaded. It was over a 4 year period I continued to smoke in secret fooling nobody but me (not even Dr. C). It had gotten to the place that on some days I couldn't even bend over to tie my shoes or even walk up 10 steps without getting short of breath literally this is no anecdote (joke) and still tends to be true on some days today. After prayer (we serve a Prayer answering God) asking him to remove this habit of 25-30yrs. from me. Saints the failure is in us not God. He did just what I asked him to do but I didn't adhere (obey) to his response to my prayer. I kept right on smoking. Well I'm about to experience my first time private room meeting that I mentioned earlier. In my private room in Trinity hospital feeling better after my shortness of breath episode (incident). Here comes that voice Y'all. Lesson to what He tells me (via the Holy Spirit). Son you asked me to deliver you from the acute habit of smoking (25-30 yrs.). I did just that, but no you continued in what you thought was pleasure. Let me enlighten (to educate) you on something. In My Holy word in particular Isaiah 55:11

it states. So shall my word go forth out of my mouth: it shall not return to me void? Saints what is God saying hear? What God is saying is that he spoke deliverance for a habit that was holding me hostage. Yet, he giving me a freedom of choice way back on Calvary I refused to adhere (obey). Somebody say" sin feels and taste good. Although it's bad for you it can feel good to you. Often when we ask God to answer prayer we want to tell him how, when and even where do it. When we should be asking him like Jesus asking him to remove the bitter cup of death from Him if such be his will. God doing it His way is not always conducive (favorable) to us. Case and point we might ask God to grant us healing. He will do it but as he sees fit not our way. Allow me to be genuinely real. When asking for a healing he might even do it by means of death. We need to realize that there is a healing in death (sorry). Think about it. Are we as human beings willing to accept his will (no) we often ask the question why. In my case here the spirit told me his word would not return to him void. I didn't even cooperate to His healing. He said my word is true. If I have to put you in the icy hands of death to make my word true I will. Oh" this was my time for a reality check. Well Saints there would be deliverance. There would be no more cigarette smoking, no more shortness of breath etc. with my illness I'm reminded of the great apostle Paul in 2nd Corinth 12 when it's mentioned about the thorn in his flesh which God would not remove but allowed him to perform his God given assignment. What you mean preacher? So glad you asked me. God hasn't healed me of this dreadful (horrible) thorn in my flesh. However just like in Paul's case he allows me to carry out his will. He hasn't changed my situation but has changed my mind set, meaning the way that I accept or receive it. He allows me to carry out his word by way of ministering, teaching or offering spiritual guidance. My Pastor tells me that I'm Gods display piece. Although I'm oxygen dependent I have never needed my oxygen while preaching a minimum forty minute sermon or expounding on a biblical lesson. I Haven't needed this oxygen supplement during or after delivering Gods word. Remember for me it's hard some days for me to even bend over to tie my shoes without getting out of breath. So to those that are going through, don't feel that they can make it or even that Gods cares. Void all of those thoughts, God cares very much and is concerned about you. Keep in mind one of my favorite scripture Psalms 30:5 (KJV) For his anger endureth but a night; his favor is life: weeping may endure for a night but joy cometh in the morning. So my brothers and sisters turn it over to God, release it and live. Thank him for what it's not for things could be a whole lot worse. Just remember "You're Not in This Thing Alone!"

My hubby Rev. C turn this manuscript over to me in the month of June 2018 two months just before his death and stated I'm through writing and you have to take it from here. I looked at him and said you need to finish this book so it will go to be published if that's what you still want to do. He stated, I can't write the last chapter(s) only you can. You know things about me that I probably can't remember or just things only you can share with the readers about me. I literally laughed as he laid the enveloped printed story of his testimony on the dining table with a flash drive. I really did not take him serious because he had been working on this writing since 2016 off and on. I happened to be home with him for (3) three months due to my own illness and shared much time together that appeared different from our 46 years of married. I guess it was because I was able to listen with my whole heart without work interruptions, family interruptions or even phone interruptions. We had breakfast lunch and dinner together everyday and were able to have real quality time together. When I look back over the numerous years this time seem so special and much discussion about our future together. He seems to want to at times talk about death and dying. I would listen and not listen you know what I mean. As a healthcare worker for 46 years I am an eyewitness to these topics everyday. Therefore, I had learned to hear clearly and on some occasions not be that attentive to protect my own emotions and feelings. It had been over 18 years since Rev. C had learned of his illness COPD and having a double heart bypass surgery due to the latent stages of this horrific disease that claim the lives of many Black American males yearly. Rev. C as he describe his medical issues that continue even after the surgery of course worsen over the years with being compromised to wearing oxygen everyday at first. He went through cardiopulmonary therapy programs to help regain strength and rehab to a new normal. Oftentimes, he would be very angry and depressed after all this was over 18 years. He spent many hospitalizations and sick days even at home trying to beat this habit. There were times he wanted to throw the towel in and stated to me "If I gotta live like this with oxygen as my partner the Hell with it."

AS HIS NURSE WIFEY

When he would have those mental depressive moments thank God for His Word embedded within Rev. C. I would just say lets Pray About It and he loved to Pray so he would be renewed to start all over again. Numerous times I could feel that he didn't Want to Pray but he never would let me down because he knew it would strengthen me too. It would be difficult sometimes to work 12-14 hours with sick patients and then come home to another sick patient who was my husband. Yet, God would remind me of our commitment to the marriage vows for sickness or to death do we part.

We had only two days to prepare our children and families that he was having a big Major Surgery coronary double bypass that could possibly take his life because of the other co-mobidities that was present from smoking over 25-30 years. Rev. C had never been in the hospital or sick in his 51 years. Our primary doctor Dr. Walton

MD would often tell me to ask him to at least get a yearly physical so there would be baseline information if he ever become ill. He had a fear of doctors and always found a reason not to go for the appointments. Yes, of course I would be frustrated as a wife and a professional health care worker who family members you constantly fought with to stay healthy. Our children and grandchildren was brought to the hospital the 2nd day evening to learn what was going to happen to Papa C.

The cardiologist Dr. Jones was so professional and demonstrated by drawing on a stuff heart with white canvas what arteries were block and how the procedure would be done. We were watching for the children's responses but actually they took things very well even after the cardiologist explained the risk factors. Rev. C appeared relieved when he saw the looks on the children and grandchildren faces that it's going to be alright. The children were taken home and I spent the night with hubby for support. It was a long night it appeared and so many tests and pre operative measures kept us both woke through the night. We both dozed off for about an hour then burst through the hospital door was a team of about six people with a crash code cart. His nurse asked what were you doing just now and we both said at the same time "sleeping" The nurse stated we have to call the cardiologist because you went into atrial fibrillation and that's not good. Shortly, the intern on called came and told us that Dr. Jones want to move the surgery up to 6:00am rather than 12:00 noon. My heart started to beat fast because realizing this is very serious and my mind wondering will hubby make it through the morning or even the surgery. Rev. C look at the intern and me and said what does all of this means. The resident bluntly stated "You're a Walking Time Bomb" and within minutes Dr. Jones his cardiologist appeared and stated I came on in because you're scaring me and you appear not to be in distress at all.

At 5:30am in the morning the surgical team was at the door of his room to escort him to surgery. Hubby was placed on a gurney and off we went on the elevator and he grab my hand in which I know reality set in for him. I started praying because I wanted to burst and cry but trying to remain strong for him. I walked with the staff as far as the pre surgery suite and it was stated this was as far as you can go. I kissed him and we gave each other the thumbs up as promised to signal he was alright. Another nurse and chaplain escorted me to the ICU waiting room where information would be provided of the progress of the surgical procedure. This is when I had my ugly cry by myself and was frozen to that seat in ICU for the next 3 hours. It was within an hour the staff came to tell me the surgical procedure was going well so far and if I needed anything. I had managed to stop crying and call the children with the update of the procedure. While sitting there waiting a lot of things was going through my mind like what if something goes wrong and if he dies. I started to realize that Satan was trying to place fear within me and I started to talk loud to myself and tell him to get away from me. I declared My hubby will and shall live in Jesus Name. I looked at the clock in the ICU waiting room and it was exactly 3 hours later. I started to get nervous and say to myself if they don't come and tell me something in the next 30 minutes going to find someone to provide an update. After, twenty minutes surprisingly it was the cardiologist Dr. Jones who appeared and told me the surgery itself went well but his concerns was Charles breathing was too rapid to remove him from the ventilator. We would have to wait over the next 24 hours to wean him off and his oxygen saturation appears (WNL) within normal limits. I was somewhat relieved but knew hubby still was critical condition due to remaining on the ventilator.

It was shortly when the nurse came to get me to view him in recovery. I went into his ICU cubicle and he looked very gray colored and seem to be struggling to breathe with the endotracheal tube. He was thrashing back and forth and I touch him to tell him to calm down. I looked at the cardiac monitor and observe his heart rate increase to 200 and I was talking to him to calm down. I noticed he kept moving his fingers as if he wanted to write something. I asked the nurse for a pad and pencil and placed in his hand and hubby started to scribble something. The Nurse said what is he doing and I remembered that he promised me a signal that he was doing okay. He drew a disfigured heart shape but I knew what it meant "I LOVE YOU" and all was well. Once, I told everyone in the room what he wrote his heart rate started to decrease and he calmed down. The nurse asked me to step out so they could really evaluate his breathing and report to the hospitalist on duty. I went back to the waiting room and contacted the children and my siblings to provide an update. The hospitalist came within two hours to state hubby's breathing was still a concern and he had failed the weaning test. I was very nervous at this point and just started to pray most of the night. I had doze off and relieved it was for a couple of hours. I jumped up from my seat and was going to head to the ICU cubicle to see if there was any progress. While in the hallway I recognize a gentlemen and it was Rev. Colin Smith a Pastor of one of my dear colleague. He asked me why I was there in the ICU waiting room and I shared with him what was happening to my hubby. Pastor Smith said, lets go to see him now and pray over him. I asked the Nurse at the desk could this Pastor and myself go in to Pray for my hubby. At first, she was a little hesitant but soon agreed; we went into the cubicle and Pastor Smith immediately begin to Pray and ask God for Healing within his entire body, every vessel, every organ, and that the blood of Jesus would bring healing. I could see life returning to him his color became pink and his breathing slowed down and heart rate decreasing. The Nurse came to assess Rev. C and ask to leave us at this time because they needed to clean him up for the next shift. Rev. Colin escorted me back to the waiting room and we shortly chatted because he was there to see a member of his congregation, too. I was so tired with this emotional roller coaster over the past 24 hours. I placed my head back and nodded off suddenly I heard footsteps running down the hall coming toward the ICU waiting room. I jumped up and went to the door and the

Nurse got to the door and told me to come with her right now. My heart was in my shoes and I felt light headed and the nurse open the door of the entrance into ICU and my hubby cubicle curtain was pulled closed. I started to scream out and said No! No! and the nurse inside the room opened the cubicle curtain back. Rev. C was sitting up in bed and the endotrachial tube was gone and ventilator was off. He said, "I LOVE YOU' I'm okay. I nearly passed out at his bedside. The Staff told me he extubated himself (meaning he spit the tube out) and started to breathe on his own. All I could say was Thank You Lord and I hugged him so tight forgetting about his bandages on his chest wall from the surgery. It was great news and a feeling of relief I contacted family and close friends to share this outcome.

Rev. C was downgraded from ICU to return to the telemetry unit for further care. He was a miracle and over a total of 4 days we were released home. Do you know after this double bypass heart surgery he only took extra strength Tylenol for pain the entire time. Who really has a big major surgery like this and don't receive narcotics for pain.

CARDIAC REHAB TRAIL

He was scheduled for cardiac rehab but did not want to go he felt it could be done at home. After, a month I discuss with him the importance of cardiac rehab therapy was to strengthen the heart muscle and promote good circulation for healing. He was focused on doing this process on his own and when he felt ready. Nonetheless after eight weeks he was not making any effort to go for cardiac rehab. Therefore, I sought to get him a puppy that would force him to take walks daily while in training. My niece contacted me that she was moving and would have to give up her dog a Shih Tzu was named Skye. I went and pick the puppy up from the groomer and presented her to hubby which really became his service dog. He and Skye bonded very well and the relationship push him into cardiac rehabilitation. He walked the puppy three times a day beginning 30 minutes and increased to 1 hour walks for blocks. He faced many mood swings throughout the six month process even depression. I would have to notify the primary physicians of the mood swings that often would be unbearable for both of us.

The cardiac rehab therapy program usually helps you deal with activities of daily living and enhance lifestyle changes that will improve your overall health. Hubby started to do very well with building cardiac reserve but started to experience increase shortness of breathe with activities. Therefore, it was recommended to include pulmonary rehab as well so his oxygen levels could be monitored more closely. It took stamina to keep him focus on these lifestyles changes on a daily basis. When cardiac and pulmonary rehab programs are moved to outpatient in the home there must be motivation exhibited by the patient. There definitely had to be a mindset change to want to be better. The goals would be explain to him to concentrate on strengthening muscle endurance, strength and flexibility. The pulmonary rehab program focused more on improving the quality of his life especially with this lung disease COPD.

LEARNING TO LIVE WITH OXYGEN

Rev, C was told Your body just cannot live without the oxygen you breathe in from the air. But if you have lung disease or other medical conditions, you may not get enough of it. That can leave you short of breath and cause problems with your heart, brain, and other parts of your body Oxygen therapy can help. It's a way to get extra oxygen for you to breathe. It was explained to him that oxygen is a prescription medication. We don't look at oxygen as a drug.

Oxygen Safety

We had to learn about usuage at home and safety measures. I was afraid to have oxygen at home because he was still secretly smoking. Oxygen is a safe gas when used correctly but we knew it's also a combustible. We had to maintain these safety tips around the house.

- Never smoke, and don't let others light up near in the house. Keep away from open flames, such as matches, cigarette lighters, and burning tobacco.

- Signs were to be placed throughout the house and we kept 6 oxygen cylinders at all times as backup.

- Stay 5 feet away from heat sources. That includes gas stoves, candles, lighted fireplaces, and electric or gas heaters.

- Don't use flammable products like cleaning fluid, paint thinner, and aerosol sprays.

- Keep oxygen containers upright. Attach them to a fixed object so they don't fall over or regulator meter don't come off.

- Remove certain materials with oil, grease, or petroleum. That also goes for petroleum-based creams and ointments like Vaseline on your face or upper chest.

- Have a fire extinguisher close by. Let your fire department know that you have oxygen in your home. My baby brother and n laws who were

Fireman would frequently look at the house safety smoke alarms and carbon monoxide detectors.

- We had to alert the electric company of usage of an oxygen concentrator so we could get priority service in case of a power failure.

We had to learn about living and traveling with oxygen because there was a need to get back to normal living. We planned and went on numerous trips that we had to prepare ahead of time for oxygen to be delivered. I can remember vividly our very 1st trip to New York City to see the opening premiere of Oprah Winfrey in "The Color Purple." We went on the train that took fourteen hours normally but the train was delayed in Syracuse for three hours. He was very concerned because his oxygen concentrator tank (liquid oxygen) started to read low. Oxygen was already delivered to the Central Park By Suiteness Hotel because the hotel clerk contacted us when it arrived. Once we got to New York we learned of a transportation strike with cabs so we were trapped at the train station. We contacted the hotel and they could not make transportation pick up due to the strike. I alerted the fire department that Hubby would run out of oxygen per his concentrator reading soon. The fire department sent an emergency team to evaluate but the problem was they didn't carry liquid oxygen only gas cylinders. They offered to take us to the nearest hospital emergency room if he needed oxygen for shortness of breathe. The concern was we needed to get to our hotel where the liquid oxygen was delivered. The ambulance could not transport us because not considered an emergency. I walked outside the train station to see if anyone was offering a livery cab service and not one person. Two hours passed and within the train station we sought to get lunch and heard over the television in the lobby that the cab Strike was over. Praise God we were given Favor once again and we ask the bellman attendant if he would flag us down a cab. We arrived at the hotel which was not very far from the train station and went to our room where we saw the oxygen was already delivered. We filled his oxygen concentrator up to the top and planned our evening to see the Broadway Theater Play. We were very excited about our first trip together with learning how to maneuver with the oxygen. Later evening we arrive at the Broadway Theater only to learn that our seats were not available due to over booking. They asked that we come back tomorrow and they would try and get us seats. You know that didn't sit well with us and Rev. C step forward to the theater window glass and ask to speak with a manager. I could literally see invisible smoke coming out of his head. I start praying and said Lord we didn't come this far to leave us now! This week vacation was a birthday present to me from Rev. C over Christmas. We had never gone away on vacation from our family during Christmas. Therefore, the Supervisor came to the window to tell us they were sorry and Rev. C told them we are miles away from Chicago; he was on oxygen and unfortunately could not come back tomorrow. They told Rev. C we could be book for the following week and boy did that send the chimney on the top of his head smoking for real. The attendant stated let me just go check seating again and return and told us there were two seats availible but not our same seats. When we followed the attendant the seats were up front near the orchestra pit and stage. How about that for FAVOR we received better seats that originally purchased. My hubby said being oxygen dependent has paid off by granting us a prividleged to have VIP seating. We just smile at each other and through the play notice that Felicia Fields which was my cousin wife was playing Oprah in the New York Broadway Play. I was just screaming then for sure that God had been so merciful. We stayed in New York a week and had a fantastic experience looking at Lady Liberty in the middle of the harbor. We went on a boat cruise to Ellis Island return to land touring Harlem, the Empire State Building and even touring the Huxtables house where the Bill Crosby Show was filming. The weather was a little cold but not bad and very little snow. We also visited The Times Square Church downtown that Sunday where a 300 Voice International Choir was having a Christmas Musical. We we're blessed with up front seats because hubby was considered for handicapped seating with the oxygen. He was smiling and said well this is different he was feeling better about accepting his new normal.

There were other trips to Atlanta, Florida, and San Diego, California. While in San Diego the pilot came from the cockpit to tell us we were a danger on the plane due to the liquid oxygen being a combustible. I told the pilot that was known ahead of time because we were returning home and the airlines was informed early. We were approved coming to San Diego and now a problem returning to Chicago. The pilot insisted that we could not get on the plane with the oxygen which was a flammable and risking others lives. I was so angry because the approval was given as long as it was not a large volume and in a safe concentrator tank. I knew my Hubby could tolerate at least 6 hours without his oxygen. I went to the bathroom and disposed of the liquid oxygen and came back and told the flight attendant to tell the pilot it was discarded. The pilot came out and tried to say the concentrator empty tank could not be place on the plane nor in the baggage car. He wanted us to not get on the plane and find a way by mailing the concentrator home. I asked for a higher authority because this was not right. Rev. C was getting upset and trying to keep him calm so he wouldn't need the oxygen. Finally, after us holding up the plane for one hour and a half they let us on and place the concentrator tank under the seats. This was very frustrating yet scary I told them this situation was going to be reported publicly. I had made proper reservation that was approved and we arrived to San Diego without any issues. Now, we're being held captive with trying to return to Chicago delayed an hour and a half this was certainly embarrassing. The lesson learned from this was to consult with his primary physician to take Rev. C off the liquid oxygen and convert to a gas or battery operated concentrator and it was granted. We return home safely and even took other short trips with our church family to Rockford, Indiana, Michigan, Wisconsin, Danville and even Arkansas.

LEARNING A NEW NORMAL LIFE

One of the most important things you can do for yourself is also one of the hardest: accept that things are forever changed. What was your normal way of life is, sadly, possibly or probably gone forever. You had to accept your new normal, which might be easier said than done. Yet, this was a new lifestyle for me as well to keep Rev. C encouraged to continue to enjoy life as best as we could.

Guard Against Depression

Many people with chronic illnesses and permanent disabilities also experience depression. It's not hard to see the connection between the two. A serious illness might result in the loss of mobility or independence, it might require special accommodations, or it might make doing once-enjoyable activities difficult or impossible. The more a chronic illness disrupts your life, the more likely you are to have a bout with depression. Maybe more than just a bout it appeared.

Though any illness can bring on feelings of sadness, the realities of some chronic illnesses and disabilities can trigger episodes with depression or long-term experiences with it. While many resources are available to combat depression, including therapy, lifestyle changes, and medications, developing a positive, tough mental attitude provides a good foundation for combating depression. It might even help prevent depression from getting a grip in the first place.

Grieve

Part of acknowledging your illness or disability is acknowledging what you have lost. You are grieving and this is a hard process, but it's an important one. Walking through grief will allow you to move on to the next stage. Not only have you lost what you had in terms of health, mobility, abilities, stamina, etc, you've also lost the fantasies and wishes you had for your future. You imagined goals and dreams for yourself before your illness. Those are now change.

Changed Life

As hard as it seems to do, you need to accept your new normal, your changed circumstances, and find fulfillment with the many gifts you still possess. Although your illness or disability has undeniably changed your life, *it didn't end your life*. Accept your condition and move forward, not only for your own sake, but for the sake of those who care about you. This was often a real struggle for Rev. C and me. However, in order to do this, it's important that you have gone through the grief process. Acceptance is the final stage of the process.

It's natural to deny a reality you don't want to be a part of. You need to accept that your old normal is just that: the way it used to be. It was a past lifetime. Holding onto hopes of what could have or would have been, can set you up for failure, disappointment, and bitterness.

Fighting the acceptance of your new normal is an invitation to fall into a battle with depression. Denying your new normal, or waiting for your old normal to return, is hard on you and those around you.

Changed Relationships

A dramatic disruption in your life causes a disruption in the lives of people around you, too. That's not anybody's fault. The dynamics of your relationship with friends, family, and co-workers might change as part of your new normal. Some of your relationships might have been based on doing the very things you can no longer enjoy.

Regardless, it takes mutual effort to maintain relationships, often requiring you to reconnect in different ways or on different levels. Find other common bonds. It may be painful to accept that reconnecting with some people just isn't going to work.

On the other hand, with some people, you'll find that your relationship is actually strengthened by the trials of your illness or disability. These are the people who matter. These are the people with whom you will find fulfillment.

You may need to strengthen your skills in reaching out. Reaching out to others for support is incredibly important. You may need help with simple things such as meal preparation, running errands, or caring for your children. Or you may simply need greater connection with others. A healthy support system is crucial to your well-being. If you find it difficult to reach out because you don't "look sick", fear that you're weak, or worry that you're a burden, a discussion with a therapist can be very beneficial.

A New Normal

Your "new normal" isn't just a list of what you can no longer do, that's one aspect of it, but it also encompasses all the things you can NOW do, including things your old normal never left you time for. Build a new reality with what you have. *You might develop new hobbies or past-times or a new vocation.* You might find understanding friends in a support group.

The best therapists in the world can give you all of the support you need, but *you* need to accept your new normal, nobody can do that for you. It was difficult for the both of us because we did everything together prior to health changes. Establishing your new normal might take some experimentation—it new after all. In time, you can do it.

Rev. C became a member of the Lung Association for COPD one summer he was invited to attend a boat excursion on Lake Michigan with other members who had in common this illness. At first, he would joke and say what is a bunch of Seniors who's handicapped who need oxygen going to due if the boat sinks. We are on oxygen and cannot save anybody plus all these tanks will make the boat possibly too heavy. (*Sometime, his humor came at the wrong time*) I looked at him and said stop putting negativity in your mind. You were a lifeguard for over twenty years at Park District and I'm sure your fight or flight response will kick in to save a few and yourself. He laughed and said, "yeah let me start to think positively".

He return from the trip so excited and happy he gain a few buddies that he could identify with for future support. Next, he started to look at Expedia travel website to start thinking about taking a cruise for the next vacation. The bible scripture came in my mind and it's my favorite, "I can do All Things Through Christ who strengthened me. Philippians 4:13

LEARNING UNCONDITIONAL LOVE

What is Agape Love?
(And What Does it Mean for Me?)

Our world has many definitions of love, but we most commonly think about love in a romantic sense. What if love, true love, meant more than romance? What if there was a deeper, truer, more full expression of love that could only be found in God and received through Jesus Christ?

Agape love is love at the highest level. It's so much more than we could ever dream or imagine.

The Definition of Agape Love

The New Testament Greek Lexicon defines "agape" like this:

1. brotherly love, affection, good will, love, benevolence
2. love feasts

I've also studied the Greek terms for love, especially the Greek word **agapē** which is supposed to be the highest expression of love—a pure, selfless, unconditional thing. But as I meditate on the love I've experienced, examining how it shaped and reshaped me, even **agape** seems not enough to explain it.

Rev. C was in and out of depression oftentimes didn't feel connected and stated a few times did not want to live. However, going through this rough phase started to take toil on me as well. He started to have the "WOE IS ME' syndrome daily and I decided he needed help to restore his confidence. It was hard to convince him at times I loved him unconditionally in spite of handicaps. Men become really troubled when things below their waist don't operate like they want. Therefore, it was a challenge to change his mindset that everything would get better. I came home from work one evening to find him very depressed and he was voicing strongly he didn't want to live like this any more. He did not want to be oxygen dependent and definitely not be able to perform sexually. I explained to him that sex is not everything and we would wait on God to restore and renew his mind that better was coming. I stepped out of our bedroom for a second and came back and he had our 22 caliber gun pointed to his head to take his life. I started talking to him that he wasn't going to go out like this that life was worth living. I grab the telephone and called Rev. Jarvis Hanson Pastor and said, I'm standing here next to Rev. C who is holding a gun to his head. He has expressed, he no longer want to live Pastor asked me to place the telephone to Rev. C ear and he spoke these words "Elder You don't want to do that and I need you right now to put that gun down." Pastor Hanson repeated himself and said, "now but put it down now." Praise God he placed the gun back into the case. I was about to faint and was praying that he wouldn't hand me the gun because of being scared of Guns! My Dad was a police officer and he had placed the fear in us kids never to touch his gun for any reason. I did grab the gun case and took it to another room to secure it. Rev. Hanson was still talking to Elder and he seems to listen to what was being discussed. I called for an appointment to our physician to see him right away and stated what had just occurred. We went to the office and anti anxiety medications were prescribed for him. However, I took one for me too because I was a nervous wreck thinking about what could have happened. We both had to really start to look at various coping mechanisms that would become helpful; Yet, I know that God is an Awesome God that took us through this stressful and devastating phase!

LEARNING COPING MECHANISMS

1. **BREATHE:**

   Practice taking deep breaths to calm you down and relax your body.

2. **WRITE DOWN YOUR FEELINGS:**

   All of that anger and frustration can be written out, and once it is all down on paper, you feel like a weight has been lifted.

3. **CALL A FRIEND:**

   Have a couple of close friends that know and understand your situation. Call them when you are overwhelmed and feeling weak. Sometimes talking it out is all you need.

4. **GO FOR A WALK:**

   A quick walk is an easy, and healthy, way to instantly calm your body down.

5. **EAT CRUNCHY VEGETABLES OR FRUITS:**
Have carrots and grapes ready in the refrigerator, and the moment a stressor hits you, take a couple of minutes to munch on these healthy snacks. It will allow your body to move, distract your hands, and give you a moment to think while you chew.

6. **LISTEN TO MUSIC:**
I don't care what type of music you listen to; music is a powerful coping mechanism. Turn the radio up and let the words of a song speak for you.

7. **COUNT TO TEN SLOWLY:**
Taking deep breaths begin counting to ten very slowly. It will give you time to act and not react.

8. **GET A DRINK OF WATER:**
Physically doing something is a great way to cope, and taking a drink of water will help you feel refreshed.

9. **READ POSITIVE QUOTES:**
When you reach your lowest moments, positive thoughts can go a long way. Reading a list of inspirational quotes can be the hand to lift you up and out of your despair.

10. MEDITATE DAILY:

Take a few moments every day to relax and meditate. It will prepare you for surprise stress.

11. DEVISE A PLAN TO OVERCOME THE STRESSOR:

Life is unpredictable, and you might be hit with a trigger at any moment. On a piece of paper, write how you will overcome this stressor when it happens.

12. EXERCISE:

Go for a run or to the gym to boost your energy and fight off unwanted urges.

13. START A NEW HOBBY:

This is a fun way to boost self-esteem and build new skills.

14. GO TO THE LIBRARY:

The library is a safe, quiet place where you can relax while checking out books.

15. CLEAN:

Cleaning distracts the mind while completing tasks.

16. JOIN A CLUB:

If Wednesday nights is the hardest night of the week, join a club that meets then so you don't have to get through the night alone.

17. START A PROJECT:

Painting a bedroom, building furniture, or working on an old car are some of the projects you can turn your attention to whenever you need a break.

18. FACE THE PROBLEM:

While coping mechanisms can be good for the mind and body, sometimes the healthiest thing you can do is face the situation. Train your body to complete a task to relieve stress, rather than avoiding it.

19. DONATE UNUSED ITEMS:

Clean out that closet or crowded garage and donate items to Goodwill and other donation centers. It always feels good to organize a cluttered shelf, but giving to others feels even better.

20. VISIT A FRIEND OR FAMILY MEMBER:

Hanging out with people is a fun way to enjoy the night and allow stressors to pass.

21. GET HELP FROM A PROFESSIONAL:

A counselor is a safe person you can talk to who will never judge you. You can express your emotions, talk about your weaknesses, and help create healthy coping mechanisms together. Hard times happen to everyone, but with the right tools, you can learn to deal with them in a positive way.

By Michelle Conway

SUPPORTING CHILDREN, GRANDCHILDREN, GREAT GRANDCHILDREN

Papa C as all the children, grandchildren and even great grandchildren AFFECTIONALLY loved to call him by that name. He had a special love support system with THEM All!

His offspring's. Papa C. would text three and four times a day with most of the children on a daily basis. He would often ask me questions what's going on with this one or that one if he had not received a text message or phone call from the children within a week.

"Papa" took his position being A Good Father in the Family very seriously as a mentor, disciplinarian and for sure role model to others.

Children

Felicia, Arletta, Tanyanika & Charles II

Grandchildren

Kantrice, Keith Jr. Kristopher, Kyle, Oshe, Tyra, Taniya, Tasia, Tempest, Tyainne, Juvonte, Nautika, Ashanti, and Sirvjonte

Great Grandchildren

Kyleigh, Trinity, Kayden, Kristen, Kayden, Eric Jurnee, Khloe, Treasure

Inspirational Quotes-Grandchildren

The greatest legacy one can pass on to one's children and grandchildren is not money or other material things accumulated in one's life, but rather a legacy of character and faith. –Billy Graham

"Nobody can do for little children what grandparents do. Grandparents sort of sprinkle stardust over the lives of little children." Alex Haley quotes from BrainyQuote.com

"Only through love will we find our way to create a world worthy of our children and our grandchildren." Laurence Overmire

Godchildren

Eugene Vinson Jr, Micheal Morris, Rev. Richard Boone Jr, Karielle Barker, Shay Shay Winston, Antonio & Zena Crossley, and His Favorite Hair Stylist Johnnie Akons

HIS CHILDREN SPEAKS!
LOVE EXPRESSIONS
TO
OUR DAD

Children, obey your parents in the Lord, for this is right. 2"Honor your father and mother" (which is the first commandment with a promise), 3"that it may go well with you and that you may have a long life on the earth."...
Ephesians 6:-1-3

PAPA C LOVE FOR HIS CHILDREN

Lady Felicia Hayes
(Daughter)

Dear Daddy,

Since the very beginning, you have always been there for me. You've always made me feel safe and loved. You were the one; I could count on when I was being bullied at school because of my size. You dried my tears, and tried to teach me to fight (hahahahahaha). You said, "The bigger they are the harder they fall." Even, as an adult, those days at work that didn't go well, I would call you crying and you would say, "Who's bothering my little big girl-Do I have to come up there?" That always made me feels better. When, I had my accident in 1979 and couldn't attend the school field trip without a chaperone; it was you who accompanied me. You made the entire day about me. After, the field trip you surprised me, took me downtown to Marshall Fields and we had lunch in the Walnut Room by the Christmas Tree. Daddy you were my superhero, my first love, and my best friend. What more could a girl ask for.

Daddy, you taught me so many things. You taught me how to love myself. You taught me that I could do anything I wanted, if I put my mind to it. You pushed me to always be the best that I can be. You taught me how to clean, even the faucets shined. You taught me how to use tools to put things together, and take apart. That's why I'm so handy!! However, I let Keith do it so his feelings aren't hurt (hahahahaha).

I remember daddy those Sundays we didn't want to go to church but stay home with you and watch the Lone Ranger and Family Classics on channel 9. I remember when you tried to teach me to step, you tried and tried. And at the time I was like daddy, nobody dances like that. Boy, do I wish I learned. Some dances never go out of style and stepping is one of them. I remember picture day and mom was at work and you had to comb my hair. OMG, I ended up with your infamous one-ponytail. Needless to say, I wasn't a happy camper that day!! When you got up in the morning to go to work, you made sure that I was up for school and ironed my clothes.

I loved the conversations where we just confided in one another. People say that I am spoiled, I say, that I am well-loved and extremely blessed to have had such a wonderful man in my life, that I call daddy.

I miss you everyday!!!

Love always,

Your Little Big Girl!!!

Forever and Always #1 Daddy's Girl

PAPA C LOVE FOR HIS CHILDREN

Arletta Conaway
(Daughter)

I was the middle daughter child who was considered that these children are usually excluded, possibly ignored or outright neglected due to the birth order. But that was not the case with our father all of his girls were "Daddy's Girl" and you we were going to be held accountable for your actions. Dad allowed us to be ourselves more than our mother who was stricter with "Baptist Doctrine House Rules" that was adopted in the family early and unbreakable. My relationship was straight up with my Daddy until I decided to walk away and do my own thing. My Daddy even gave me one on his cars and I loved working on that car. He knew I would cherish and take care of it versus my other siblings!

When Dad got sick it was hard to see him not able to do the things he use to do. I could even see the hurt and disappointment in his face when he said to me 'Buba' you know I cannot do that anymore, so I am going to need your help. Which I can semi relate because as I continue to get older there are something's, I cannot do any more as well and I find that as being a bummer.

Dad was called to minister it was kind of like a 'wow' to me considering my Dad is a quiet person and does not seek attention. I know to be a minister you must stand in front of a congregation and deliver the word. I went to his first sermon and yes that was another 'wow' lol seeing my Dad on the pulpit speaking to a crowd of people. This I know he was stepping out on faith because this was not his comfort zone.

When I got that phone call from my mom at around 7:00am in the morning; I so remember it until this day I screamed to the roof top awakening my neighbors. We both cried on the phone until she could gather herself to tell me to get there. I was so scared to enter the house I seen family members going in and out it took me awhile to even enter the home; I was in disbelief and still am because it does not feel like he is gone. I know he is not here physically because I do not see him. I do not know, it's hard to explain how I actually feel some may understand where I am coming from and some may not. One thing I do know I miss talking and joking with him. I miss you Dad!!

PAPA C LOVE FOR HIS CHILDREN

Tanyanika Conaway
(Daughter)

Reverend Charles Conaway, my daddy, my first love, my texting buddy, my laughing partner!! It's so much I can say about my father. Growing up my daddy was mean lol but he meant well and didn't take no stuff from nobody!!

I remember all the road trips we've taken my entire childhood, we went to different states almost every year and daddy drove to everyone of them! My father was my rock, my go to person when I was in a storm and didn't know which way to go!! We had our own bond that no one could ever break, of course not lol I'm His baby girl!! Bible questions I had I run right to Papa if he couldn't find the answer or didn't know he would simply say BOO T BOO DADDY DONT KNOW SOMETHINGS ARE A MYSTERY AND DONT

WORRY YOURSELF TRYING TO FIGURE IT ALL OUT, I know you're a over thinker and you want answers some things just can't be answered!! I love you daddy always and forever!!!!

PAPA C LOVE FOR HIS CHILDREN

Charles Conaway II
(Son)

First off, I want to give Honor to God who is the head of my life and to my outstanding parents. I'm going to get right too it, when I think of my dad it's sometimes unbearable knowing I will never or neither see him again with human eyes nor touch with physical hands. My dad was a very approachable person that you can talk about anything too, It' funny because after you spill your guts to him he going to ask so what you gonna do. I can tell from how he says that how I'm gonna handle the situation. I and my dad didn't always see eye to eye but when we got on one accord we had an unbreakable bond where we would often discuss the Bible and Sunday School Lessons. Our relationship went from not talking at all to him being the best man in my wedding, now that's the power of God.

It's so much I can say but I would probably have to write another book. Last but not least I want to thank my mom for being patient with my dad through his sickness and being there through every tear he might had shedded. I was granted to talk to my dad the night before he passed, we was talking about my son being diagnosed with leukemia and how things was getting unbearable for him, I never thought in a lifetime that would be my last time talking to him, so as the scripture says Life is like a Vapor here today and gone Tomorrow, I salute you Dad and will never forget you continue to rest you well deserve it Love you your Son Earl.

RELATIONSHIP WITH CHURCH FAMILY

"TABLE TALK Among Friends As Family"

Best Brotherly Love

Elder or Conaway that's how I answered the phone when he called me or I called him he was a special guy to me definitely a BFF. We talked once or twice a week anywhere from 45 minutes to an hour maybe I enjoyed more talking to him I would come up with a question pertaining to the Bible and if he didn't know the answer then he said bro I'll look into that and get back with you. Lo and behold the next day or later he will give me the answer. Oftentimes, the answer would lead us into a debate on the topic or send Elder back to research for more answers. He was the guy that I feel really was good to talk to about any and everything. I did enjoy and the best part about talking to him he did not hold back; he would always tell me the truth and give me his opinion too. I can honestly say he was always on track he encouraged me to read the Bible more which was always something I had a hard time doing because it unusually put me to sleep. I really really really miss that guy just the other day I was going through and I needed someone to talk to and I had no one. This has happened to me quite a few times and it's a lonely feeling. There's one thing about him I notice he would have his oxygen tank sometimes near. Conaway would have his oxygen tank sometime as he was teased carried it for decoration because he would sit it on the side of me or lay it down. He would have a pretty bad cold at times and would reach and put the oxygen on. Yet, whenever he got up in the pulpit to preach I noticed that he would never use it to deliver his message. Also, when he finished the message he didn't need it to me not really signs of shortness of breathe to warrant the use. He was one of the few ministers that I know and felt that was truly a Man of God. When he called me and told me to pray for his great granddaughter that she was born with heart problems. I really started praying for her and told Elder I'll call you back. I would often call him back and ask him how the little Princess was doing. He hadn't told me her name Elder just said pray for her so I just started calling her that name. I felt honored when he called me and asked me to be his

Great granddaughter God Father. Let me rephrase that he called and told me that I was going to be his great granddaughter's God Father only Conaway. I guess that's the type of relationship we had and understood each other. Our relationship started with us going downtown to a steakhouse that I cannot think of the time at this time but it was on Wells Street. Needless to say we never made that happen I often think about that mission wasn't fulfilled. God Bless you Brother see you soon and rest in peace much love.

Deacon Craig Harvey!

DEACON LUCIUS & ESTHER PATRICK

Rev. Conaway was a friend and he was someone we looked up to and admired him. He was fun to be with and most of all very spiritual. He truly loved the Lord and whatever he said something he would back it up with a scripture to encourage you. He would always stop and Pray with You when times were difficult and when he knew you were concern about something. Even though you could hear laughter in his heart there was seriousness in his mind. He was the type of person who wanted to be by your side because he was faithful. We love him as a friend, as a man of God and as a Brother. Rev. C would Pray with me and my wife. I was his Best Man at his 25 Year Anniversary renewing of the Wedding Vows. Also, just a good man, friend and Godly Man. We would talk weekly and he was there when the death of my 1st wife and he helped me through the grief process. I enjoyed the many church vacation trips with Rev. C and we would eat meals together. We were on the

Deacon Board together and went to serve members of our church their communion every 1st Sunday. He loved the Sunday School and would call and discuss the up coming weekly lessons. Rev. C would drive to Bloomington to visit he and Dr. C and we all would go and dine at Red Lobster his favorite seafood restaurant. He is truly missed!

DEACONESS BARBARA EASTERLING

Let me start off with his favorite scripture:

For his anger endureth but a moment; in his favor is life; weeping may endure for a night, but joy cometh in the morning - Psalm 30:5).

You can't think of or hear this scripture without thinking of him. If anyone could own a scripture, this was definitely his. Though not by blood, he was my Big Brother. It's funny how we were joined together by my son and I will forever be grateful for his selection in choosing his godparents, when it's usually the other way around, but still and all we were all blessed because of it. I know he was a true confidant because I've never heard anything I ever told him in private ever repeated in public. He was truly one of God's angels and one of the kindest souls I knew. He chastised me lovingly when I may be out of line with some of my thoughts. He praised me as well when he saw change in me for the better.

He would call or text me often and tell me his spirit told him I needed a kind word, encouragement or to just pray for me. He would never ask what was wrong just following the spirit. I would sometimes call him and tell him I needed prayer and again, he would never ask why, he would just start praying. I truly miss those moments and especially our exchange of food pictures (mostly from Red Lobster Restaurant). I think at one time we were in competition to see which of us visited the most. He was truly the best at being a great friend, brother and godfather in my life and will always be remembered for his strong faith and tenacity in helping anyone, spiritually or otherwise that he could. We had so much table talk among our group but it was always in love and full of laughter,

Love and miss you my brother.
Barbara Easterling

DEACONESS LYRA CRAWFORD

Brother and I met at new Nazareth church he was on the Usher Board and I was on the Nurses Board we both worked for Pastor JE Hopkins brother was his Usher an armor bearer. We became good friends in the office mostly laughing and joking and teasing one another for certain things that we did in the office sometimes if we ran late I could come in and he would tell me go comb my hair and I would tell him go wash your face and we would laugh that was a lil joke between the two of us. When he was elevated to the role of a deacon I missed him sorely my partner was gone we worked well together taking care of Pastor Hopkins. He was no longer in the office with me yeah we still remain close friends I'd love to purchase him word search puzzle books he could work those things so fast it would make your head swim so I prided myself on finding WORD search puzzle books that were big and hard to do he would still call me up and say aww ha you must have thought you had me when he was ill I would try to make sure he still had his book I would go to the hospital to visit him.

At church we would sit together in the dining room for dinner and we would tease each other about the way we ate sometime. We would laugh so hard and loud that our spouses would look at us as if though we were crazy and say to us alright Y'all. Brother loved to tease me and I would to tease him. When we got in trouble we would point at each other and say that's him /her.

He would often tell me things that he desired to do as would I to him we had a way of encouraging each other into doing some of those things. When he was cool to preach he would look at me and asked me was he sure I would tell him if the Lord brought you to it; he will take you through it but we will just wait watch and pray. We always pray one for another and our conversations would always stay with each other. That was my brother I loved and miss him dearly.

Brother when you see this go wash your face smooches and yes I will comb my hair. Smooches

SISTER SANDRA DRIVER

I brought humor and laughter to the table talk after church services usually arriving more for the broadcast afternoon services at 4:00pm. My husband and I would drive all the way from Bloomington, IL where we resided. We loved coming back and forth to Chicago as often as we could because we loved our church family and Pastor Hanson.

Rev. C and I had an inside loving bond because he would always call me to ask why wasn't my husband and I not at church. We missed a few Sundays because of work schedules, illnesses and because we had to drive a two hour trip coming and going. Rev. C would inquire so much until it made us create a love bond because he would take the time and call us if we did not make it to church. I began to call him my Personal Pastor because even through his illnesses he took the time to check on my family. Oftentimes, I would surprise Rev. C and our conversation went just like this.

Me: Good Afternoon my Pastor!

Him: Good Afternoon How are you doing Sandra and Walter?

Me: OKAY! How are you Pastor?

Him: You have been excommunicated from the table because I haven't seen you guys in 2 Months

Him: Where's Your Tithes and Offering?

My Pastor I call Rev. C would definitely call and check on me and my husband all the time just to let me know that we were missed and that I have not been to church Yet be sure to send my Tithes and Offering!

All I have left to say is We Miss You My Pastor Conaway Friend!

Sandra & Walter Brown

MOTHER VERNITA LARRY

Memories of My Loving Son Child

He was one who loved the Lord who gave of himself and shared his services to them he came in contact with. He was never too busy to take time with you or just provide encouraging words. He just represented Love and His personality always showed the Love of God to others; A True Messenger of the Savior. A Man of Standards who lived what he taught and believed. He was small in stature but tall in the Love of Christ, Church and His Family. One who will Always be remembered who will Always be My One and Only Son Child. Who I Loved!

From Mother Larry!

RELATIONSHIP WITH SIBLINGS

Rev. C was the baby in the Family of five which there were two girls and three boys. As he stated earlier he was adopted at a very early age and grew up as an only child. He later rekindled his relationship with his siblings as an adult after the death of their oldest sister. He later experiences the death of his father, grandmother and eldest brother suddenly at the age of 44 who was the Dean of Students at Columbia College. The oldest brother's death was tragic for the remaining siblings that experience allowed the last three siblings to pull together and restore the family relationship.

Harold (Brother)

Uncle Harold as everyone calls him would visit our home every Friday when he would fly in town from St. Louis while working for TWA airlines. He and his brother would chat about work, the kids and of course Rev. C would always ask him when he was coming to church. It was notice that question would shorten the visit until next time. Harold has four children, and five grandchildren. Rev. C and I would encourage him to allow the kids to meet their cousins. He would start to open so that this generation would visit each other and experience social events together. Harold finally retired from TWA and moved back to Chicago and over time started to experience health issues. We were called one afternoon to an emergency situation where Harold was found at a Bus Stop and it appeared he suffered a stroke and was hospitalized. He came to lived with Rev. C and me until he could rehabilitate to return home. His brother was able to return home and function well to activities of daily living. It was about 10 months prior to Rev. C passing his brother had suffered a severe stroke this time with other health issues. We made numerous trips to the hospital and would assist with his children a health rehabilitation plan for recovery. Harold health began to fail drastically and he was placed on life saving measures and Rev. C was summoned to making decisions for terminating life. This took toil on Rev. C to see his brother health worsen and it began to really affect him. We visited Harold in Intensive Care two days before the unexpected death of Rev. C. We decided not to tell him that his baby brother had passed away until he was better.

Margaret (Sister)

Aunt Margaret as most calls her is the only sister alive of Rev. C who has experienced numerous health issues too. She was placed over thirty plus years ago on life support not expecting to live. Numerous emergency codes were called over a six to eight month timeline where the doctors wanted the family to remove life support but yet she made it through. Now, Margaret lives in Colorado with one of her sons who is a Pastor. Oftentimes, Rev. C would mention he wished that they had a closer relationship earlier in life. Yet, she loved and formed a bond with her baby brother and would speak with him over the phone during certain occasions. He was elated when he looked out into the congregation and saw Margaret and Harold sitting when he delivered his first message. I had kept it a secret that they both would attend his first sermon. Margaret has two sons one in Chicago and the one in Colorado which is in the ministry. It was a tough time when I would have to contact her about both brothers being very ill around the same time. She decided to come to Chicago when Harold health worsened. Rev. C was glad that she came to check on them but she rushed back and did not spend anytime with him and he was a little upset. Margaret called him several times afterward and he seemed to feel better. However, on Friday Harold was placed on the ventilator and the doctors wanted family to make a decision for Do Not Resuscitate (DNR). Rev. C decline and said we're all going to Pray and Wait on God. It was heartbreaking and shocking when I made the called to her that (Charles) brother had just passed away in his sleep. She thought it was Harold and I had to tell her no it was baby brother.

LIVING A HEALTHY LIFESTYLE AND BE HAPPY

Rev. C everyday challenge was finding ways to live healthy and be happy after being told on the death experiences from his doctors. In so many words go home and while living be preparing to die. I have often heard various ministers say "We are leaving the world of the dying going to the land of the living." There would be several mornings where he couldn't even put his shoes on less known tie the laces without experiencing a severe decrease saturation of oxygen. There were numerous trips to Trinity ER for exacubations episodes due to COPD arriving with oxygen levels that were below normal limits 84%percent and lower. The physicians would start to ask me what works for your hubby and when Rev. C could begin to speak he would tell them what the medical regime needed. I watched him so many times frustrated, disgusted, overwhelmed but he would always manage to let me know he loved me. He was so humbled and loved the Lord and trusted in him for living a healthy life as he possibly could. After a few days of the medical regime steroids, nebs treatment, antibiotics prophylaxis and CPAP at the bedside he would begin to minister to other patients, nurses, doctors whoever came through that door. He really did not need a pulpit or platform because it was in his heart to reach and preach the gospel of Jesus the Christ.

Rev. C would leave the hospital and the physicians would just shake their heads because he was alive. I remember the ER physician at University of Chicago told us he was afraid of Elder because he didn't know what was keeping him alive. He had experience at this point about five life saving measure events, over 15 hospital stays and 8 various surgeries including Double Bypass Heart surgery with over 80%percent blockage and going to work everyday with no symptoms. I was unhappy in preparing healthy meals, reviewing healthy programs to build cardiac and respiratory reserve. I was to the point to just say Lord Jesus how ever you Bless Elder I will be satisfied. He was placed in the Arms of Jesus to work His Plan for his Life.

It was one month before Rev. C death I was called to a job in Atlanta to work for a huge multisystem hospital. I was in an orthopedic boot due to Achilles Tendon Tear. I was summoned to interview the very next week. Elder said,

You should go ahead an interview and I will be just find. I didn't feel that comfortable going that far without him plus; I had that darn boot up to my knee. In addition, we were a little scrap for cash due to medications not covered under the insurance, co pays and me home sick for 3 months. The secretary at the hospital in Atlanta, Georgia contacted me a 3rd time to come interview. I explained my dilemma and she said let me call you back. She called me back in 30 minutes to tell me she booked airline tickets for Rev C and me to come to Atlanta for the interview. The hospital security chauffer would pick us up at the entrance of the airlines and escort us to our hotel. We laughed because we both were in wheelchairs at the airport one couldn't walk and the other couldn't breathe. Next morning the chauffer was in the hotel lobby at 8:00am to take me for the interview that was going to be held all day. Rev. C went to the lobby with me and the chauffer said you can ride with me to take her to the hospital I will bring you back to have breakfast. We both looked at each other and just smile because we knew God was in Control! The interview process went quite well and we return home safely. I received a called in two days and they wanted me to relocate immediately. This was a short notice and just didn't feel it was the right time. Rev. C so considerate and kind told me to go and he could come later. I was floored and was just on cloud ten that he was always thinking of me. He was such a Provider for his Family for 35 Years employed at the well known Flagship Store Marshall Fields. He started as a stock boy in the Walnut Restaurant and worked his way to Systems Administrator for the entire downtown store. He was brilliant yet remained humble to serve God's people. He was Mr. Customer Service in that store he was even chosen to represent Marshall Field in there ambassador mentoring programs for Youth Teaching and Speaking on "Customer Service." Marshall Field was known for the quote "To Give The Lady What She Wants" by any means necessary to keep her Happy! Ya'll guess what this Lady Got What She wanted 24/7 (Spoiled) by him. His Black Queen!

I decided not to take the job because it was a huge undertaking in a short time and I could not leave him or my family at that time. I needed to focus on keeping him Healthy to fulfill the Plan God Had for Him!

PASSION FOR TEACHING & PREACHING THE WORD OF GOD

When a man is called of the Lord to preach, preaching ought to be the passionate pursuit of that man. Jeremiah wrote, *"But His word was in mine heart as a burning fire shut up in my bones, and I was weary with forbearing, and I could not stay"* (Jeremiah 20:9). Every preacher understands that passion to preach the Word. However, passion is not sufficient by itself to consistently provide the teaching and preaching God's people need. It must be blended with elements such as purpose, planning, and preparation to edify the saints and to enable them to build up the ministry. Per Dr. Mike Edwards

Rev. C. had a burning passion to teach and preach the Word of God. I would watch him study constantly week after week. He wanted to be prepared when called to reach God's People. Numerous sermons were written weekly and stored in a portfolio in his library office space. He would research topics and review definitions of words as he would tell me (exogenesis) the text. Most of all he would Pray everyday that God would humble him and feed him the message in order to "Preach Jesus." He always sought for the approval of his Pastor Jarvis J. Hanson who he admired and often would mimicked eloquent words he heard such as "perigaphy" "Sermonic Dissertation". He loved this Young Joshua who was a preaching machine and Rev. C. wanted to be available and prepared once called upon. When he was made aware from Pastor Hanson he was going to Preach he would Rest, Pray and Study every day for hours to reconnect with God for His Message to deliver. I admired his steadfast and preparation skills to always be ready. I believe many of the other Ministers would be jealous on how the Lord would use him In Spite of His Handicap! God would show up and show out and take over and allow him to Preach without his oxygen and not need the oxygen afterwards. I knew that was the Holy Spirit speaking through Rev. C because we would go home and sometime he could not even take his clothes off due to shortness of breathes. Elder would talk most of the night through his oxygen mask and treatments on how good God was to him. I know God use Rev. C as his display piece to show the world to just abide in me. I was to the point of not being frightened or wandering what was next because God had his hand of grace and mercy placed upon him. Praise God for His Mighty Acts of Loving-kindness to take Care of Us Until the end as He Promised!

Elder was a die hard for Sunday School aka (D.C.E.D Hour) he would start reviewing the lessens before they were to be discussed. He would study through the week with his only Son Minister Charles via telephone, Deacon Patrick, Deacon Harvey and conclude with Superintendent Deacon Vertis Short who both challenged each other to really prepare for the lessen so if there would be any questions from the students. Oftentimes, he would want to comment on the Sunday lessen even when he had an episode of shortness of breathe. Rev. C felt the lessons studied should hit the teacher first then they could teach effectively to their students.

I recently started to read this book entitled "Women of the Word" by Jen Wilkin and the book tells us How to Study the Bible with Both Our Hearts and Our Minds. The author of the book stated on pg. 19 "for those who are ready to face squarely the mountain of their fragmented understanding of Scripture, and brandishing a spoon, command it to move." She discussed valuing the 5 P's of Sound Study: Study with Purpose, Study with Perspective, Study with Patience, Study with Process and Study with Prayer. It was stated that the order was not the focus but each of the 5 P's supports the others: we pray for patience to study well. Perspective and process are intertwined and rely on keeping purpose in view; Bearing in mind that all five P's are equally necessary and interrelated. Yet, each of these vantage points will help us begin to grow in Bible literacy, training us in the exercise of mind-before-heart. God-before-self. (pg. 46-47) This passage made me reflect back on how Rev. C would prepare himself and stay ready to move whatever mountain he faced knowing God Reign in his life.

REV. C EXPRESSESS GOD'S GOODNESS TO HIM THROUGH BACK TO BACK TRAILS & TRIBULATIONS MESSAGE

(Excerpt from message he delivered)

One Minster by the name of Rev. Reed often states the fact there is no need to go way back into yester years to know God has been good to you. I can just go to 2016. I'm not starting from January but from July of 2016. July 7th the unexpected death of a dear friend of ours. August 3rd massive flood in our home. August 4th an automobile accident. Two weeks later Dr. C incurred a bad stomach virus. November 6th experienced a horrendous (awful) fire in our second home. November 14th I had emergency surgery hospitalized until the 22nd spent 6 days without food or drink. November 19th great granddaughter three weeks old becomes very ill coded placed on a ventilator. In the month of December again unexpected lost another good friend (we shared the same birthday) and a step brother passed. Well less I've keep you too long. Let it be known that the God we serve is able to keep us. Just like He told Paul His strength is made perfect in the time of trouble and His grace is sufficient. If it had not been for the Lord on our side we could and would have lost our minds. He didn't change our situation but the situations kept us dependent on him just as he did the apostle Paul. Just as he declared on that Sunday morning he has all power in Heaven and on Earth.

God bless you Pastor Hanson,

God bless you New Nazareth and God bless you my brothers and sisters in Christ.

LOVE EXPRESSIONS

FAMILY & FRIENDS

It is often said that love conquers all, that love is the greatest force in the universe. It is the force that gives healing and life, binds souls together, and whispers to us that all will be well. We can see throughout the Bible that love conquers fear, evil, and sins.

SUPERINTENDENT. DEA. VERTIS SHORT & JUNIOR SUPERINTENDENT ANDREA SHORT

(Father & Daughter)

Rev. Conaway was a mild-mannered gentleman with a confident stride. He always had a kind and encouraging word for everyone he encountered. One could be sure to engage in a good, hearty laugh with him on occasion.

The man of God took his prayer life very seriously. He would "go to the Throne of Grace" with such passion and fervor, I would sometimes worry for his health. If a prayer was to be delivered to Heaven, I believe he was definitely one that could do it. During service, it was fascinating to see him compelled to leave the pulpit to pray specifically for someone in the congregation.

During Sunday School class or even in Teachers' Meeting, Rev. Conaway enjoyed studying God's Word and sharing his insights. The knowledge he shared was most appreciated and helped to shape everyone's understanding of the lesson at hand. He could always relate the lesson back to real life, for he was rather transparent about his own experiences. I recall how he demonstrated this in a sermon he preached in October 2017, highlighting Psalms 23:4. He explained that the shadows referred to in this Scripture can be any problems or tough situations we face. But one of the lessons Rev. Conaway concluded with was: "DON'T JUDGE MY BREAKTHROUGH UNTIL YOU KNOW MY GO-THROUGH!" That statement certainly resonated in our lives.

There is so much more that could be said about Rev. Conaway, but I'm especially proud of THIS great accomplishment in becoming a published author. As an avid and voracious reader, I am super-excited about a new book to read. Dad and I can hardly wait for the completed work, for it is one that will be cherished forever.

Thank you so much for allowing us to participate in this undertaking, for Rev. Conaway was very near and dear to our hearts.

REV. KEITH BARKER & KIM BARKER

(Husband & Wife)

Youth Ministry

Hi we're the Barker's and I need you to understand that an experience with Rev. Conaway It was truly an experience. First my wife would have conversations with Rev. Conaway and every conversation was always a "Sermonic Dissertation". No matter what how small it was for an example a song he would want to hear, he would say I need to hear this Particular song and the crazy thing about that it would be on the list to be sung that Sunday.

As for my life I always knew that God hand was on me, but this Particular day I was running late for church but and being late I believe it was all part of God's plan. I walked in the door the first person I saw was him and I spoke to him saying "Good Morning" Deacon Conaway and knowing I'm a deacon he responded be saying Good Morning Reverend Barker and I'm not taking it back. Then something ignited it in the Spirit rim that morning I answered my call to God it was like he had a direct connection with God. He will truly be missed we love your spirit go ahead and take your rest......

Rev. Keith & Kimberly Barker

EVANGELIST BARBARA JAMES

(Sister N Love)

O my God! What can I not say about "This Precious Man of God" truly an amazing brother n Love, a friend, an encourager, a Man of Great Faith, a phenomenal Trooper! I loved our talks, he would say Elder! Hallelujah! I missed him so, loved my sweet Sister! Dr Glennell Conaway, a family man, his children and grand's his heart! I thank God for sharing Him with Us for many seasons, Joy, happiness and laughter, fun, he loved Us all! He's Our brother! "Chuck" Rev Charles Earl Conaway! Made his impact with all of Us! Just everyone! A Saved Man! Spirit filled!! Prayer Warrior! Missionary! Wise man, he Preached and Lived! I love my Bro n Christ! Hallelujah! Thank you Jesus! For his Life! My bro and friend! "When Nita would bring his sour dill pickles he would say now sis don't take nothing but Two" Glory! Hallelujah!

MINISTER CATHY JACKSON

(For His Glory Prayer Line Ministry)

Pastor Conaway was very instrumental to our daily prayer line ministry,

Every first Friday of the month we would have a guest preacher come and share the gospel of Jesus Christ with us. Pastor C, would always have fresh manna from Heaven above. He would always take his time to make sure that his messages were very clear and concise; he rightly divided the word and made sure every angle pointed us back to Jesus Christ.

Pastor C, had a love relationship with Christ, it was very evident in his teaching, he was very passionate about the word of God and he made it known to many. He was a regular guest preacher on For His Glory Prayer line Ministry. He lived a life worthy of his calling, his faith was impeccable he truly believed. He was an awesome witness for Christ.-

Love
CJ (God's Girl)

"It's All About MEE Giving GOD The Glory!"

REV. KEITH HAYES, PASTOR

Son N Love
(The Gathering Worship Center)

On November 12, 1989, Charles E. Conaway Sr. handed me his little girl. Even though we all know that no one will be ever good enough for their little girl. I guess he figured, what's the use in fighting it, it was what his little girl wanted. And whatever she wants, she gets. In our receiving line he looked at me and gave me a smile and this big hug! We're family now! I had heard that in-laws don't get along, so I was preparing myself for a future life of constant "in law" conflicts.

However, my father in law soon became "Dad" in every true sense of the word. But even more than that, he became my friend, we would just hang out together; my running buddy, visiting the sick and shut in, attending and officiating funerals and burials (I bought him his own personal "funeral" flag for his car);my project assistant engineer, we were "wrecticians", either we were going to fix it or tear it up trying; nurse practitioner, when I would have respiratory issues he would give me breathing treatments; my study pal, we could expound on the scriptures together; my prayer partner; and my confidant.

I'm forever grateful to my wife Felicia and her siblings, Arletta, Tanyanika and Charles for sharing their Dad with me.

SIS. ALTRICE WARD

(Sister Friend 40 Years)

It seems uncanny, God, how many times people have been placed in my life at just the right time, with just the right words of faith, wisdom and insight as I struggled with the experiences of life. I can't help but believe that somehow, Lord you had a hand in putting this man in my path of life. It makes me feel special that the Lord would bother to arrange such a person as "Chuck" to have specific and meaningful moments of time with him in our many conversations over the years. Lord, I just want to let you know that I am grateful for knowing this man of God, named Charles Conaway or "Chuck" and the extended family that includes me also. Thank you for bringing us together as a family. And He will be a gift to me that will be treasured forever, and a part of our hearts forever.

REV. COLIN & DR. NELLIE SMITH

(Redeeming Grace)

My friend: Reverend, Preacher, Evangelist Charles Conaway

It has been a great privilege, honor, and joy to have met Rev. Charles Conaway, miraculously through my friendship, sisterhood connection, and job-related association with his darling wife, Dr. Glennell Conaway. I will hasten to say that to know Rev. Charles was to love him. It is also an honor to share a tiny part of this manuscript, which he authored, yes, and a legacy of a lifetime. As a special friend for many years, I gleaned and did recall some very precious moments. His wisdom was extraordinary, and he was prudent of the decisions that he made. I remember Rev. Charles for his firm stance for holiness and righteous living, purposeful fearing God, passionate about God's Word, sound in his Christian beliefs, strong in Faith, and was a preacher of the

Word. He was a strong man, a good man, a kind man, and he was indeed my special friend.

Rev. Charles was a model husband, dad, grandfather, great grandfather and friend who encourage, assists, listens, and he was a great communicator. As I recall further, there was never a dull moment when in his presence. His laughter was distinct, and his smile was contagious. As a friend from my close relationship with him, I learned many life lessons that I will always embrace. Rev. Charles faced several health-related issues and formidable challenges here on earth, but he never one day complained or thought or life mistreated him. He was a terrific listener, a great evangelist by a message he preached through his life and the soft-spoken biblical truths even when his challenges got hard.

His care and concern for others were often demonstrative of his life. During my tedious journey of writing my dissertation, it was sometimes challenging to commute to and from campus. Rev. Charles often volunteered to assist me with getting to school when he took his wife, Glennell, to our evening/night classes. The loving moments shared, along with many encouraging words to my entire family, will never go unnoticed. Humility and love for people are trademarks of my memory list. His passion and appreciation for his wife, Glennell, his nurse, caretaker, and his lover, his best friend, were always mentioned with gratitude that sometimes his expressions sealed with a manly tear.

He was my friend indeed. He talked about life's issues, his journey with chronic illnesses, but he would seemingly see the hope at the end of the tunnel, always thanking God for his life, family, and for being alive. The title of his book, "Don't judge my Breakthroughs until you know my been through." A survivor can only pen it. Rev. Charles was a man who had his share of trials along the journey called life. However, he wrote as confident that his thoughts will come to an end when Christ, his redeemer, would grant him permanent breakthroughs.

My special friend Rev. Charles, I promise you will harvest and cherish those precious memories you left behind. The best things in life are the people we love, the places we have been, and the memories we have made along the way. As long as there are memories, they live in our hearts forever. Your life was a blessing, your memory a treasure, lived beyond what words can measure.

Humbly submitted,
Nellie A. Smith, MSN, Ph.D.

REV. LEVAN & LADY JEWELL BRAYBOY

Pastor Emeritus

Rev. Conaway was a very faith filled Man of God. There were many occasions when we would break down the Word of God over a meal. A lot of times we could not finish our food because we were so full off the WORD OF GOD and happy. Rev. Conaway was a fun person to be with. He would always keep me laughing and he met nobody as strangers. One thing I will never forget about Rev. Conaway was that he said what he meant and what he meant what he said. I Pastor Emeritus Levan Brayboy will always cherish our Spiritual Bonding.

"HE WAS FOR REAL!!"

JUVONTE JOHNSON CONAWAY

(Grandson Over Comer from Leukemia)

My grandpa was a great man to be around with. He always knew how to make you smile and laugh. I could call him and talk about anything I was going thru he had the best advice. He was always positive but didn't take no mess. I ain't ever seen him angry at the world even though he was battling demons. I really look up towards him a lot. He gave me the courage to battle hard against my cancer at 17 years of age. He didn't give up on himself so why should I have, but he passed the day after finding out about my Cancer struggle. That's why I will always love and remember all the good times I had with him. He was a soldier and always believed I was.

Love You Papa

TYIANNE CONAWAY

(Granddaughter)

I always had a habit of closing myself off from the rest of the world, and sadly to say, that also included my family. I never called when I was supposed to, was never really into family events, and got lost in my own little world. As I got older I felt this shift inside of me to be more active in the real world and by the time I realized that it was too late. The more I was away the faster my memories faded until there was none. The only memory I have saved in my files of Papa and I is us sitting on the couch, him talking about how much he loved Skylar (Shih Tzu puppy), about how she was his little baby, and him telling me not to tell anyone because they might get jealous. I guess that is why I asked my Nana for Skylar when Papa died. I took her in, to have a piece of him that I didn't cherish when he was here, to remember that love he gave her, and to remind myself to reciprocate that love to others.

~Tyiann

DEA. JERRY MADISON

(Deacon)

Life and friendship of Charles E. Conaway, Sr. What can I said about Rev. Charles E. Conaway (aka) Chucky as I would call him. I can say that Rev. Conaway was a man of God. I can remember when Rev. Charles Conaway was the late Rev. Dr. J.E. Hopkins personal usher and would carry and put on Rev. John E. Hopkins cape on him. Charles Conaway became a deacon of the New Nazareth Missionary Baptist Church with other deacons and served well as a deacon. He was preaching as a deacon in services. I was there when he got the assignment to become the Prayer Director. Charles could pray a whole hour without stopping. I witness this to a fact on one Tuesday night prayer meeting. Afterward I told him man you going to need that oxygen tank to catch your breath. I remember when Chucky received the called to the ministry. On Sunday,

May 1, 2011 Rev. Charles E. Conaway, Sr. preaches his first sermon from St. Matthew 27:32 "Must Jesus Bear The Cross". On Another Sunday March 30, 2014 Rev. Conaway preach his favorite scripture Psalm 30:1-5 "His Anger Is Only Just A Moment" I would always get a phone called from Chucky ask me how my brother is doing. I wanted you to be Dr. C. Uber's driver and take her down town to take care some business. Those were the days that I treasured to be asking to take him or Dr. C somewhere.

DEA. RONALD HALL

(Brother N-Love)

Was I his little Brother?

Was I his Son?

Was he my other DAD?

Was I his Friend?

When my sister married this guy, I may have been in 3rd grade and he immediately bonded with me. He let me walk with him to Howard Cleaner's on 47th street to take my sister's reception dress to get ironed. He let me help out at the open bar at his wedding reception. I thought "man he's cool and he looked like the BLACK James Bond in that tuxedo". WOW!!! What an impression........!

As I look back at that time, that was only the beginning of many GREAT IMPRESSIONS he would leave to me to cherish and to behold as if I was apart of the vows he had made to my sister.

As his life went own he exemplified what a man should become.....A (big) brother: Webster says one related to another by common ties or interest and teaches his siblings about life values...HE DID THAT!

The (other)DAD, Charles(Chuck) carried some of the same traits that my real DAD(Saul) had so that I have no EXCUSES; provider, hard worker, discipline, LOVED his family, LOVED his wife and LOVED what GOD had done and was continuing to do in his LIFE....HE DID THAT!!

I remember as a kid Charles (Chuck) took me to a Halloween show at the State & Lake theatre. The opening act started out with a magician with card tricks. As the show went on it became scarier and scarier.....a big needle going through a guys stomach, a head getting cut off, a lady getting cut in half. By now I'm under the seat shaking, covering my eyes begging Charles to get me out of there. He finally took me out of there. Fast forward 30 years, We were talking about that Halloween night and he told me "Ron I was glad you said let's get out of here...I was SCARED and under my seat too"

So as I got older and witnessed an example of a REAL

MAN, A REAL DAD…..I finally understood THAT he was my FRIEND, my BROTHER, and my other DAD…

So, If you wonder why I SOAR, HE was apart of the WIND that GOD put beneath my wings!!!

DEA. ANTONIO & MINISTER ZENA CROSSLEY

(Son & Daughter Friends)

I have many things I can say about Poppa Conaway. When I first met Pop Conaway as a child, I didn't know he would have such an impact in my adult life. Although Pop Conaway had 4 biological children of his own, he was a father figure to me and he always made me feel like I was his own. Poppa Conaway had many Godsons, but I always knew I was fortunate to be one of them. He was never too busy to pour into me and my family lives, whether it was through prayer, conversations or just listening. After talking to pop I always felt encouraged. I love the way he would say Son. Nobody could say "Son" like Poppa Conaway. Pops continue to rest well in the arms of the Lord, knowing that your legacy will live on through me and many others.

Lovingly Antonio and Zena

REV. TYRECE HUNTER

(Nephew N Love)

A great man is reflective of the inheritance he leaves his family. Uncle Chuck, as we formally called him, a man full of quietness but loud as a roaring locomotive. This man embodied every aspect of God, Family, and Love. Although he would come off as the grumpy older man, this was just part of his character. This man was the first to speak into my life about ministry and promised to purchase my first Bible when it came to fruition. Today, I carry that Bible with me everywhere I go.

As a child, I fondly remember going to their house and having the time of my life. Aunt Glen would make the famous family taco salad, and the cousins, and I would eat and play. Uncle Chuck would come around with his frail frame grumpy about all the kids in the house but would take time to speak and rush upstairs to his room.

Uncle Chuck spoke life into me when I felt afraid of men, I was never intimidated by him because of his small frame, but something inside me knew that this man meant business. My Aunt loved him dearly, and it was reflective in their time together. You never saw one without the other. I applaud Uncle Chuck for his support of my Aunt as she was the family scholar. She went to school all the time and had so many accomplishments because of her home support system. Although those she walked the stage to get the degree, I strongly feel his name should be on each because of his unfailing love and support for the love of his life.

ELDER VERNON COLE

(Nephew N Love)

Stoic! That's a word that easily comes to mind when I think of Uncle Charles. It means *a person who can endure pain or hardship without showing their feelings or complaining.*

Now I don't like to reminisce about him as being acquainted with his exterior conditions only, but there was such an interior steadfastness that he maintained in contrast to the turbulent storms he had to endure, that you can't help but mention the darkness to emphasize the light.

Having become a member of his family through marriage, most of my conversations with Uncle Charles came when I was in my thirties. These talks were never long or drawn out, but they were warm, full of optimism, and sincere. I was growing and maturing as best I could in marriage and fatherhood, and he was resolute and experienced in both. So I valued his perspective when I'd see him on holidays or at family gatherings, and there was no greater testament to the man he was than seeing the love and high regard that his family, and especially his wife and children, held him in. Whenever we did get opportunity to share, he would always lead with how thankful to God he was, in spite of his many trials, and from the first conversation until our last, I never once heard him complain.

In this way, I saw him like a seasoned knight from medieval times. Even though his experience had earned him the right to be surveying the battle from the hill, the undaunted man, wearing a weathered and battered suit of armor, always chose instead to face his enemy at the front, in the heat of the battle, alongside his comrades. This example left an indelible impression on me, and I'd imagine, upon everyone that he came in contact with.

Uncle Charles will always be, to me, the epitome of strength.

SIS. DEYANNIE WASHINGTON

(Niece)

Uncles are a gift from God. Words could never tell the joy an uncle brings. Uncle Chuck and I have a special bond. He was very caring, understanding, kind, funny and had an abundance of love. You could talk to him about anything, and then suddenly he would remember to ask me "Did you have your bread today?" He and I loved bread; it really did not matter what kind either. His love was unconditional, to the very end. As he watched me grow into a mom, wife, sister, niece and the list go on, he always would let me know how proud he was to be my Uncle. I watched him and admire him as he mastered being a supportive husband, father, uncle, grandfather, minister, and then great-grandfather. He did things without complaining even until he got ill. He mentioned all sickness is not unto death and reminded me to live life to the fullest but keep God first. Uncle Chuck will always have a special place in my heart.

Until we meet again, Your loving niece DeDe

REV. DAVID BALLARD & LADY DONISHIA BALLARD

(The Word Church Rockford, IL)

The definition of strength varies; it's not just about being physically strong. When I think of Uncle, as I called him, his bravery in dealing with this last season of his life was an example of strength. The strength of a man. One who carried an oxygen bag wherever he went but never complained. The strength of a man. One who was determined to preach the gospel of Jesus Christ while carrying that bag. The strength of a man. One who showed us what trusting God looks like. The strength of a man. One who encouraged others as he himself was going through. The strength of a man. One who I never heard complain about the hand he was dealt. The strength of a man. One who never stopped smiling and laughing. The strength of a man. One who's laugh was contagious. The strength of a man. One who supported my husband and I to the fullest no matter how many miles apart we were. The strength of a man. As we looked from the pulpit both him and Auntie were waving. The strength of a man. One who would make me sing whenever I was in his company. The strength of a man. One who could eat and loved him some bread. The strength of a man. One who was the same every time you seen him. The strength of a man. One who I'm sure knew my name but ALWAYS called me niece. Uncle, your living was not in vain. LESSON LEARNED! We love you!

Lady Donishisha Niecy

There was no question that Rev. Charles Conaway was and still is a great inspiration to me. When I started my pastoral journey in 2010 he was there and He visited my church at least once a year. While that may not seem like much, it was major to me because of two things that I'll never forget. One time he and Auntie surprised us on a Sunday morning. It was a hard Sunday for me but I still had to preach. It was something about seeing those two in the pews that gave me the motivation I needed to get through the sermon. After church Rev. Uncle Charles grabbed my hand and said, "I'm inspired!" Wow Rev! He had no idea my struggles that day, but was able to be inspired by what I'd preached. Little did he know that that statement alone has pushed me through some tuff times in ministry. The last time Rev. Uncle Charles visited our church was in 2017. We'd just bought our building and he & Auntie drove up to celebrate with us. I took them on a tour of the building and needless to say they were very happy and excited about what God had done for us at the end of the tour I said to him, "Pray for us so that I can pay this mortgage off within five years." He looked at me and said, "You don't even have to worry about that....I'm speaking it! And you're going to burn the mortgage well before five years!" Even with all of his physical challenges he was a great inspiration. He never gave up; never stop going, never accepted defeat. WHAT AN INSPIRATION!

Pastor David Ballard II

REV. COREY D. LEWIS, PASTOR

First I thank you for allowing me to be apart of this amazing venture.

My relationship with Rev. Conaway feels like I've always known him, he's has been a father figure as well as an advisor. Rev. C was a man of faith as well as a man of purpose I remember him being the lead servant of the prayer meetings and that showed me his dedication as well he knew he had a calling on his life. Rev. C is missed greatly I will always hold our talks highly and will also remember what he stood for. It's been said our life on this earth is just for a moment, make it count Rev. C made it count he was dedicated to God his family and friends. Rest on my brother.

"LIVE SO THAT ALL WHO KNOW YOU BUT, DON'T KNOW CHRIST WILL WANT TO KNOW HIM BECAUSE THEY KNOW YOU"

From the pen of **Pastor Corey D. Lewis**

SIS. JENALE KING AKA STAR

(Nurse Practitioner)

Rev C!! My Uncle Chuck!! You were one of my greatest supporters always giving me words of encouragement. You chastised me with love; you've given me pointers as a teacher of God's work. I will never forget and I can still hear you say "Star put the notes down and let God use you!! I took that and stamped it in my heart. Rev. C was a great role model as a husband. He taught me not to settle and wait on who God has for me. He talked me thru several anxiety attacks via text messages. Uncle text messages were so timing!!

Rev. Conaway was an individual that thought of others above his own illness. Oftentimes, he would be in the emergency room waiting to be admitted to ICU or the transitional ICU where I worked as a Nurse. I would help oversee his care as a patient and family. When, other Nurses would provide care for him he would tell them that's my niece and she will get you all if you don't take care of me jokingly. He would want certain foods that wasn't on his hospital menu and would insist I get different foods that he really likes. I would tell him going to tell Auntie that he was acting out. He would look at me like no don't get Dr. C. involved then he would act right! I am just glad even on frequent flyer visits many opportunities came for me to assist in his care when he was hospitalized. Lastly, I cherish all the love shown during our talks which could be about anything he would respond with good sound Christian advice.

Love You and Miss You Star!

REV. DARRYL REED

(Associate Minister NNMBC)

Rev. Conaway was a good friend down through the years if he did anything for you he never told anybody.

We went to the Chicago Baptist Institute in class together sitting next to each other he always make sure because he would say you know I can't hear. He loved people and cared about humanity always praying. Sitting next to him in the pulpit he kept you laughing. Sometime his wife Dr. Conaway would look up and laugh herself because she knew he said something funny. I will always remember him as a Loving Brother as a Deacon, a Preacher and Director of the Prayer Band on time if it was nobody but him I really miss his encouraging words rest well my brother last but not least he was a great friend and he loved my Mother Mrs. Ora Lee Sansom.

SHIRLEY VINSON

(Neighbors 35 Years)

The Vinson's and the Conaway's were neighbors and friends for over 35 Years, live (5) five doors down from each other. We both had (4) four children (3) three girls and (1) one boy child and coincidental both husbands had the same birthday. Eugene and "Chuckie's" friendship grew as brothers from another mother. They spent hours together on their off days and discussed family issues, manly issues and would have a beer or two. These two buddies smoke cigarettes while visiting in the backyard and when the cost went up $3.00 dollars it convince both to quit for a while. Both of these guys had so much in common. They love their Daddy's Girls and were very strict about their circle of friends. Chuck would work six days a week including Sunday's for at least 25 years while leaving every morning at 7:00am Eugene would yell out the window "Not to make All the Money." Leave some for him especially doing holiday seasons.

Eugene was a CTA engineer and would work many hours too so when they visited each other they've talk for hours. In addition, Eugene was handy with fixing cars so both would get under the hood of their cars to compare notes or whatever. The Vinson's were our neighborhood watch guards and if anything happened they would keep the Conaway's informed. Both of our families would attend the block club parties and on holidays cook foods and barbecue to exchange meal plates by the end of the day. If our families would have any emergencies you could count on both these Men of Valor to cover for each other. Our husbands were the best of friends the Conaway's became our Son Godparents as well. When learned that Eugene passed away he was heartbroken and made a vow to continue to support and check on the Vinson Family.

DR. MANDAKINI POKHARNA

(Primary Care Physician)

Dr. Mandakini Pokharna was Rev. C primary physician for fifteen years who basically provided his medical care until his death. She had grown to love and care for him. They both had a bond where she could really read his mental state of mind and would ask him questions and allow him to verbalize his feelings. He would enjoy going for his visit with her because she would take time and ensure he was comfortable to follow the medical regime. A few times he would disagree with the treatment plan but she would always allow him to tell his side that was not agreeable. When she went on vacation Rev. C did not want to see any other doctors because he knew they would ask too many questions. When he would have days that appeared dark or heavy she would do breathing exercise with him in her office until he would release the feeling before leaving.

Dr. Pokharna would call Rev. C at home even if it was not a clinic day just to check in with him. He enjoyed the attention from her and would comment that he was her special favorite patient. She would tell me that Charles would make her feel better because he would tell her about His God. Dr. Pokharna told him on several occasions will you Pray to your God for me because you have a spiritual connection. This would cause Rev, C to smile. In addition, she encouraged him to start to write about his experiences throughout his many health challenges because other people with this illness could learn from him. Dr. Pokharna was a blessing to him because she always encouraged him to live to the best of his ability and not allow life issues to take away his inner Joy!

SPOUSE

(Wife)

I was contemplating if words of love expressions were in order for me to write in Rev. C manuscript because it's about him. Nonetheless, I told myself there are other wives that need to hear from you on how to express love beyond measure. Learning to live the marriage vows that God ordained not what man writes for themselves. When there is a paradigm shift that stresses the love between married couples you really need an understanding of what helpmeet means written in our Bible. It was 46 years ago I married my Soul Mate and our love was inseparable until death. I certainly did not see it coming those latter 20 years of the marriage when the health challenges that would test my faith and end with an eyewitness testimony.

Charles as I knew in the beginning of our life together we became 8th grade sweethearts. It was interesting how we met through a City of Chicago (NYC) Neighborhood Youth Community Program that provided various jobs. We were hired as young tutors for children in summer camp programs. We were escorts in classrooms then as field trip escorts for various educational events such as visiting Field Museum, Science of Industry, Lincoln Park Zoo, Brookfield Zoo and Amusements Parks as far as Michigan City. I was afraid of roller coaster rides and this young man volunteered to ride with me with my children assigned on the field trip this particular day. I could tell he instantly had a crush on me but standing reservedly on my Daddy's Girl principals would not allow giving into emotions. As we started to grow as children attending high school we were separated due to different schools for two years and without exchange of phone numbers. It was a New Years Eve that there was a knock on the door of our home at 9:00pm. My mother went to the door and a young man was there inquiring entrance to see me. My mother let me know and granted him privileges to visit. It had been two hours of having conversation when my mom came to remind us it was getting late and we needed to prepare for watch meeting church services. Charles looked at my mother as she was expressing hints for him to leave he boldly asked if he could go to church with me. You know this was his lead into my heart and my family because our home was deeply rooted in the Baptist doctrine and Christianity. We became a very young couple dating and soon married that started life as newly husband and wife.

We both were working still pursuing higher educational careers to provide a rock-solid home for our children. Our Christian beliefs system was tested in the beginning of the marriage; because church was a lifestyle for me and occasional for hubby. Yet, as time went on Charles wanted to see what was absorbing most of his wife time at the church. Ladies as most men when you pouring out more time other than home it could be a little threatening to them. However, praying for my husband and home as the scripture tells us "As for me and my house we will serve the Lord" Joshua 24:15 that resonated in my heart as a goal for my family. God heard my prayers and one Thanksgiving Day while attending church who showed up but Mr. C. I was in the ladies restroom changing our baby daughter diaper and one of the Deaconess of the church summoned me to the sanctuary. My heart was bubbling over to see that my hubby had joined New Nazareth church under the leadership of Rev. John E. Hopkins Pastor. I was always taught by my parents as a girl a family that prays together stays together that still holds true today.

Mr. C became a member and Rev. Hopkins did not believe in bench members. Therefore, he was assigned to the angelic choir, then the usher board, amour bearer for Pastor Hopkins, Deacon. Next, latest elevation was as a minister under the leadership of Reverend Jarvis J. Hanson, Pastor. I watched this young distinguished gentleman over the year's spiritual life grow to a dedicated man of valor, disciplinarian in our home, spiritual mentor in the word of God, loving husband and loving friend to many. As aforementioned by Rev. C he was tested by God to promote testimony and servitude to his ministry calling. There was nothing that could separate him from the love of God as he was blessed even through many challenges with illnesses an episodic near death experiences. As a wife it was my job to Pray! Pray! Pray! And be a Servant to assist with his needs. My years of experience as a Nurse helped to prepare me for this faith journey that often push us both to the edge. There were many nights lying awake on his chest hearing his irregular heart beats and witnessing breathing apnea where he had to be shaken to wake up to restore a better breathing pattern. Ladies, I learned over the latter twenty years of married life ups and downs that true love was beyond the bedroom sheets. Sistas! you will need to learn the agape love for your helpmate and love with every fiber of your being this only comes from God above. God gave me the strength to face every battle and come out victorious every time. This scripture became my favorite, "I can do all things through Christ who strengthened me". Philippians 4:13. When Rev. C started to preach I would be frighten about him over exerting himself and reducing his oxygen levels to trigger shortness of breathe. But, as time went on God showed me that Rev. C belonged to Him and would be use as a display for His Glory! Therefore, I dared not to get in the way especially feared that God would move me for trying to stop the plan that he prepared for him. I became comfortable about God's plan for him to preach and just would be there in the pews to show support as His 1st Lady. I trusted God like Elder did and we both became eyewitnesses to what our Mighty God could do even through a man that was deemed by man to be oxygen dependent.

EXPERIENCING DEATH AND GRIEF

SCRIPTURE

Isaiah 54:10

Though the mountains may shake and the hills be moved, yet MY loving kindness will NEVER leave you, says the Lord who has compassion on you. (This means that no matter what happens in your life, everything could be falling apart to know that God loves you and is with you and will NEVER leave you)

Looking back on an experience that I would like to share sent me on a roller coaster ride of depression and anxiety and later shook my foundation four months later after experiencing the Death and Mourning of my hubby after 46 years, the love of my life, my best friend, my lover, my children's father, grandfather, great grandfather, my confidant, and was my childhood eighth grade sweetheart.

The voice on the other end of the phone stated "What's Your Emergency" while continuing Cardiopulmonary Resuscitation (CPR) I said my hubby has No Pulse and Not Breathing I'm doing CPR and no response. The dispatcher stated I'm sending an ambulance and you will have to stop doing CPR to open the door. I stated to her, I can't stop doing CPR right Now my hubby has no pulse and not breathing. I heard the emergency responder then say the response team is at your front gate stop CPR to allow them access into your house. I gave my hubby two breaths and a round of chest compressions and ran to open the door. I ran back to the bedroom to continue chest compressions checking for a pulse and the paramedic voiced ranged out to say lets us takeover Maam. How long have you be doing CPR and tell us about his medical history. One paramedic started chest compressions and another started an IV to administer rescue code medications. My hubby skin color was a gray tone and didn't have any movement or a pulse. The two paramedics picked my hubby up from the bed and place his 145lb lifeless body on their mobile cart all four paramedic ran down our hallway fast. One of the emergency team paramedic said "We will be taking him to University of Chicago hospital meet us there. I started screaming and calling out Lord Have Mercy! Lord Have Mercy! I'm Not Ready For This! Please, Lord Help Me!

Therefore, driving through the streets I managed to follow the signs on the hospital building to the New ED. I rushed inside the ER and the guard at the door stated Maam you can't go back yet. I heard him say, "The chaplain will be out to speak and bring you to where your Hubby is." I said, "No call the Chaplain and tell him that I need to be at his bedside if he's going to leave me." (in my mind) I gotta be there. I was feeling so numb and lonely with emptiness in the pit of my gut! The Chaplain arrived momentarily but it seemed like hours. The curtain was pulled around the cubicle where I could hear the clinical staff working on my Hubby still providing lifesaving measures. It was about thirty minutes when Rev. C started to show that he was responding to the emergency treatment plan.

The emergency room physician told both of us a good job was done earlier to start CPR immediately. The paramedic shared once they got Hubby in the fire rig his pulse had returned next was getting him to the hospital which made this a successful event. We both looked at each other and stated God IS Awesome! He still has worked for You to do! Hubby was transferred up to (Intensive Care Unit) ICU where Rev. Hanson visited and prayed for Elder his hospital stay was 4 days with a remarkable recovery.

Dark Clouds Appeared Just Like That

It was four months later when my heart seem like it stop beating and I was walking around robotically on auto pilot. After arriving home at 7:00am having an out patient procedure Sleep Study opening up the door to find the house alarm system was still on. My two dogs both Shih Tzu's Sky and Skylar were running down the hall to get my attention. I found it strange that they were not out on the morning walk with Hubby at this time. This was their routine everyday between 6:00am and 7:00am. I heard my Hubby breathing machine on so I said he's taking a breathing treatment. I entered the bedroom the lights were off and I could see his body silhouette lying down. I chuckled and said, "how are you laying down taking a breathing treatment." I notice no response so I said to him stop playing and answer me. I felt Hubby was being a prankster this morning then I went to turn the light on to notice his nasal mask was sitting on top of his chest and he appeared sleeping his eyes were closed. I made my way over to him and said again stop playing only to touch him and Hubby body was so COLD! I gasp and said, "Lord Have Mercy." No You Didn't Go and Leave Me especially when I wasn't here to Help You. I said in a loud voice why You didn't call 911 by pressing your emergency alarm necklace around your neck. I looked at hubby directly in the face and could notice the PEACE on his face and a GLOW to his SKIN. I threw my Hands UP In The AIR and Said LORD I ACCEPT YOUR WILL. I could hear a voice saying I was Hubby 911 response team; no more pain or suffering after 18 Years of debilitating Health Illnesses diagnosed with COPD, HEART DISEASE after having A DOUBLE BY PASS SURGERY, and PULMONARY HYPERTENTION. In addition, Hubby was placed on the lung Transplant list at Loyola Hospital after a year of work up only for the doctors to tell us he was doing so well he was removed from the list. The physician said he had over 75 percent of lung capacity to do activities of daily living. What was really more remarkable and strange to many that Hubby was OXYGEN DEPENDENT BUT WOULD PREACH WITHOUT ANY OXYGEN?

BUT GOD! That was truly the DIVINE POWER OF THE HOLY GHOST!

When your spouse dies your world certainly changes. You are in mourning feeling grief and sorrow at the loss. You do feel numb, shocked, and fearful. You even feel guilty for being the one who is still alive. At some point, you even feel angry at your spouse for leaving you. All of these feelings I found out are normal. There are no rules about how you should feel. There is no right or wrong way to mourn. When you grieve, you can feel both physical and emotional pain. People who are grieving often cry easily and can experience trouble sleeping, little interest in food, problems with concentration, and stressed with hard time making decisions.

In addition to dealing with feelings of loss, you also will need to put your own life back together. This can be hard work because you have very little energy. Some people feel better sooner than they expect. Others may take longer as I did almost two years.

As time passes, you will still miss your spouse. But for most people, the intense pain will lessen. There will be good and bad days. You will know you are feeling better when there are more good days than bad. You may feel guilty for laughing at a joke or enjoying a visit with others. It is important to understand I learned that can be a common feeling.

Make a Decision to Seek Professional Clinical Support Systems

There are many ways to grieve and to learn to accept loss. Try not to ignore your grief because I did. Support may be necessary until you can manage your grief on your own. It is especially important to make a decision to seek clinical professional support with your loss if you feel overwhelmed or very depressed by it. My under shepherd (Rev. Jarvis J. Hanson) Pastor spoke and prayed for me numerous of times. Yet, that void was still there and I even hid behind a smile knowing my heart was shattered into pieces and broken.

Family and compassionate friends can be a great support but mostly on short terms. They are grieving, too, and some people find that sharing memories is one way to love on each other. Feel free to share stories about your love one who is gone more so with people who support you. You are all trying to cope with the death of someone you cared for a very long time.

For some people, mourning can go on so long that it becomes unhealthy. This can be a sign of serious depression and anxiety. Talk with your doctor if sadness keeps you from carrying on with your day-to-day life. I slept on the sofa for a year and a half never getting into bed unless sleeping over to my children's and family members house. I really needed clinical support and prescribed medications until I could manage the grief on my own.

HOW GRIEF COUNSELING CAN BE OF ASSISTANCE

I found grief counseling helped to make it easier to work through the emptiness and sorrow. Regular even weekly talk therapy sessions with a grief counselor or therapist certainly helped me to learn to accept death and, in time, to start a new life.

Remember to take good care of yourself. You might know that grief affects how you feel emotionally, but you may not realize that it can also have physical effects. The stress of the death and your grief even will make you sick. Eat well, exercise, get enough sleep, and get back to doing things you used to enjoy, like going to the movies, walking, or reading. Accept offers of help or companionship from friends and family. It's good for you and for them.

We have (4) four children, (14) fourteen grandchildren and (8) eight great grandchildren I had to remember that they are grieving, too. It will take time for the whole family to adjust to life without your spouse or loved one. You may find that your relationship with your children and their relationships with each other have changed. Open, honest communication is definitely important. Always know that "Family Matters" has become my FB # hash tag sign.

Mourning takes time. It's common to have roller coaster emotions for a while. Yet, I thank God who keep pulling me through and most of all referring back to the scripture six words *"HIS LOVING KINDNESS WILL NEVER LEAVE YOU"* has significantly helped me.

PASTOR PREACH THE EULOGY

Rev. Dr. Jarvis J. Hanson eulogized his Son in the Ministry on Saturday August 11, 2018. The Life Celebration Home Going Services for Reverend Charles Earl Conaway Sr. was carried out in divine order. The Scriptures read were Old Testament Psalm 23 New Testament 2Timothy4:7-8 and New Nazareth Voices Choir blessed us with renditions of Elder favorite's songs such as "Total Praise," I'll Trust Him," "Every Praise is To Our God," and his favorite Psalmist Sis. Natalie Hamler McClain sung a solo, "Center of My Joy", the obituary was acknowledged of His Story in which he wrote prior to his death within this book passage. Rev. Hanson prior to providing the eulogy message presented a notable certificate of ceremony to Our Only Son Minister Charles II Ordination Papers recognizing that Rev. C would be declared officially ordained. Pastor Hanson also, stated this was just an earthy declaration but that Elder went to his heavenly ordination which was higher than what man could ever have offered on Earth. Rev. C was looking forward to this ordination he was studying his packet weekly that Pastor had provided early because the original date was to be in October 2018. Rev. Hanson came from the book of 2Corinthians 12:7 and then he referred to Psalm 27:13 I would have fainted, unless I had believed that I would see the goodness of the LORD in the land of the living. 2 CORINTHIANS 12:7 (Paul) said, "And lest I should be exalted above measure through the abundance of the revelations, there was given to me a thorn in the flesh, the messenger of Satan to buffet me, lest I should be exalted above measure." This confirms again that his "thorn" refers to the trials and temptations, which came through persecutions, not sickness. These scriptures all show that the scriptural attitude towards persecution is to rejoice, be happy, and to glorify God, which was exactly Paul's attitude towards his "thorn", confirming again that his "thorn in the flesh" was people persecuting him, and not a sickness. Therefore, Rev. Hanson preach that Elder didn't just die he laid down his life because he was ensured by God his family was at Peace and would be taking care of it was a "Solvent Discharge" referring to Rev. C was ready, he had lived through Heart Attack, Respiratory Failure, hospitalizations; he was ready to be released. Pastor stated, his coming to church Sunday after Sunday oftentimes huffing and puffing yet pressing his way through his illness. Rev. C was grateful and his response was remaining humble through this experience and accepting "The Thorn In His Side." It wasn't death from illness that took Elder out but he checked out caused he was Ready. His Family was ready and had accepted God's will and this showed Rev. Hanson that this Walk of Faith displayed helped him at this time due to his own situations he was facing during this time too. Then came Rev. C. favorite scripture that closed this message Psalm 30:5; Weeping May Endure for a Night but Joy Cometh in the Morning." Amen!

AFTERWORD

We pray that you have benefited from reading this book and will used Rev. C life lessons learned to help you through your Faith Walk. Our lives are certainly a gift from our Heavenly Father and learning to love your life is a great way you have "An Attitude of Gratitude." God knows we are not perfect and will never be perfect but we can Command Our Day and make the best of life by living the divine plan God has for each of us.

My So Beloved Hubby a distinguished christened gentleman you taught even me so much and our loved was so profound over 46 Years! The Last thing You told me the Evening Before You passed as Always *"**It's Me, You and Jesus!**" And Now I Say "**It's Me & Jesus**" Until We Meet Again*!

We all must learn to love one another unconditionally(Agape); Let us first love Our Lord and

Saviour Jesus the Christ who died on the cross so that we would have the right to the tree of life! Jesus gave his only begotten Son so we could be redeemed. We are covered with the blood of Jesus! Amen

REV. C. FAVORITE SCRIPTURE

Weeping may endure for a night,
But joy comes in the morning" *(Psalm 30:5b).*

Dear Sista or Brother, who's been crying,

I felt like the Lord wanted me to encourage you today. Because...

He saw you, the other day when you were so upset. Last night when you were crying. When you were hurt; when you were angry. He saw you. And He has not forgotten.

He sees the pain in your heart. He sees you right now. And He knows.

He knows what it's like. He knows what it's like to feel despised and rejected. He knows what it means to not have a single friend in the world. He knows what is hurting your heart right now.

And He cares.

You see, this thing that is happening to you is not God's best for you. It's not His will for you to mourn or grieve or be sad. It's not His will for you to hurt, physically, emotionally, or mentally. He loves you, and He's a good Father. He desires only the best for you in all things.

REV.C FAVORITE QUOTE

"If You Take Care of God's Business He Will Certainly Take Care of Yours!"

REV. C FAVORITE SONG

"Every Praise Is To Our God" by Hezekiah Walker

WOMEN LOVE YOUR SPOUSE AND DON'T FORGET TO PRAY! "YEARS I PRAYED FOR YOU (REV.C) THESE PRAYERS"

1. **Pray for his work.**

   "Lord, I pray that You would bless my husband's work. That he would be diligent and prosperous. That You would give him wisdom and discernment. God, I pray

You would give him strength to walk the opportunities you provide. Thank you, Lord."

2. **Pray for your husband's heart, soul and mind.**

"Father, I praise You for my husband, Your unique creation. Please guard his heart and mind, Jesus. Protect him from temptation and fill him up with the good things he needs. You've promised to fill his soul with what he needs and I ask You to do just that."

3. **Pray for healing from the past.**

"God, would You heal the wounds of my husband's heart? You've promised healing to those who submit to You. Lord, please smooth the scars of past hurts and brokenness. May Your healing permeate his being, inside and out."

4. **Pray for courage.**

"Lord, You are gracious and merciful, yet You are all-powerful and understanding. This world can be a fearful place and I pray that You would give my husband courage. Lord, infuse his character with courage for daily decisions and the difficult ones as well."

5. **Pray for your husband's leadership.**

    "God, You have provided Your Word and I am so grateful. May Your Word guide my husband as the leader of our home. May his leadership skills be empowered by your wisdom. I trust that You will lead in his hand and heart in our relationship, his work, our home, community and church."

    **"YEARS I PRAYED FOR YOU (REV.C)
    THESE PRAYERS (cont'd)"**

6. **Pray for wisdom in finances.**

    "Lord, money yields the greatest potential to cause problems in a home. Please give my husband wisdom as he seeks to honor You with finances. I praise You for the blessings You've provided and I pray that You would help him, help us, to always honor You first."

7. **Pray for a heart for the Lord.**

    "Father, please give my husband a pure heart for You. May he seek to love You and trust You with everything he has and is. Protect him from opinions intended to sway him from Your Word."

8. **Pray for his speech.**

"Father, in a day when the world speaks with complete corruption, keep my husband's words pure before You. I pray that he would use his words just as You would have him to. I praise You for his personality and pray for purposeful conversations in our marriage."

9. **Pray for your husband's friendships.**

"Lord, I pray that You would provide encouraging friendships for my husband. That he would know he is never alone because You are with him, but I ask for others to speak into his life and sharpen him as he sharpens them."

10. **Pray for your husband to be a good father.**

"God, I thank You that You are the good, good Father. Would you help my husband's parenting to reflect You? May his children know Your heavenly love personally and experience it through their earthly father."

By Rachel Wojo

PRAYERS TO MY FAMILY DON'T GRIEVE FOR ME!

Don't grieve for me, from pain I'm free

I'm following the path God has laid, you see.

I took his hand when I heard his call

I turned around and left it all.

I could not stay another day

To laugh, to love, to work or play.

Tasks left undone must stay that way

I found the peace on a sunny day.

If my parting has left a void

Then fill it with remembered joys.

A family shared, a laugh, a kiss

Oh yes, and these things I too will miss.

Be not burdened with times of sorrow

I wish you the sunshine of tomorrow.

My life's been full; I've savored much,

Good family, good times, and a loved one's touch.

Perhaps my time seem all too brief

Don't lengthen it now with undue grief.

Lift up your hearts, and peace to thee.

God wanted me now; From pain I'm free.

Anonymous

SCRIPTURE INDEX

NOTES

The Holy Bible: King James Version. (2009). (Electronic Edition of the 1900 Authorized Version., Jn 21:15–17). Bellingham, WA: Logos Research Systems, Inc.

https://www.webmd.com- Definitions

Oxygen safety- Oxygen Therapy At Home: Tips for Using Oxygen In Your Home (webmd.com)

Agape definition- Agape - Wikipedia

Learning to cope mechanisms-by Michelle Conway www.morningsiderecovery.com

Inspirational Quotes-Grandchildren

The greatest legacy one can pass on to one's children and grandchildren is not money or other material things

accumulated in one's life, but rather a legacy of character and faith. —Billy Graham

"Nobody can do for little children what grandparents do. Grandparents sort of sprinkle stardust over the lives of little children." Alex Haley quotes from BrainyQuote.com

"Only through love will we find our way to create a world worthy of our children and our grandchildren." Laurence Overmire"

Passion for Preaching and Teaching- 7 Elements of Passionate Preaching | Ministry127

Women of the Word by JenWilkin pg.39-41(written permission?)

Women Praying for Your Spouse Rachel Wojo- 15 Ideas on Ways to Pray for Your Husband - RachelWojo.com

ABOUT THE AUTHOR-REV. CHARLES EARL CONAWAY SR. (WRITTEN PRIOR TO HIS DEATH))

Rev. Charles Earl Conaway Sr. recently became an Ordained Minister of New Nazareth M.B Church for 45 Years with membership in various Ministries such as: Pastoral Ministry of NNMBC, Sunday School (D.C.E.D Hour), Deacon Board, Director of Prayer Band Ministry, Men of Valor Ministry, Amour Bearer to Rev. J.E. Hopkins, Usher Board and The Angelic Choir. He was a distinguished husband for 46 years, father of 4, grandfather of 14 and 8 great-grandchildren that had a Passion to Preach and Teach the Gospel.

Charles Conaway was employed at Marshall Field (Flagship Store) downtown for 35 Years. He held various positions such as Administrative Systems Director for entire store, Electronic Sales Manager, House Wares and Sporting Goods Manager. He served as the Ambassador for their Youth

Outreach Speaker for "Outstanding Customer Service." for Chicago Public and Private School Job Enrichment Programs

Elder was an alumni of Tilden High School, American School of Broadcasting College, student in study Chicago Bible Institute and New Greater Era Mid District Baptist Association.

About The Co Author-Dr. Glennell Conaway RN BSN MSHSA, M.Ed, Ed.D, CLSS

Dr. Conaway is a Christian and Member of New Nazareth M.B Church for 48 Years, leadership and membership in various ministries such as Women's Ministry, Ministers Wives, NNMBC Sunday School (D.C.E.D. Hour) Ministry, Deaconess Ministry and Nurses Board Ministry. She has organized numerous Women Retreats and Engage the Platform as Speaker on Numerous occasions to express her Love for Christ and Others.

Dr. Glennell Conaway has 45 years experience in the health care industry and health care field; 36 years as a Professional Registered Nurse with extensive education with a Doctorate of Education Organizational Leadership, Masters in Education, Masters in Human Services Health

Administration, Baccalaureate Degree Science of Nursing. Dr. C. is Certified in Lean Six Sigma (CLSS). She is an alumnus of Olive Harvey College, Lewis University, Spertus Institute, American Intercontinental University (AIU) and Argosy University. College Professor at Robert Morris College and Wilbur Wright College in Health Studies Curriculum and Nursing.

Printed in the United States
By Bookmasters